BRITISH COLUMBIA

ALBERTA

SASKATCHEWAN

Peace River

Athabasca River

North Saskatchewan River

Edmonton

Jasper

Cariboo Mountains

Fraser River

Saskatoon

Banff

Golden

Monashee Mountains

Calgary

Red Deer River

Bow River

Vancouver

Kootenay Lake

Penticton

Victoria

Moose Jaw

WASHINGTON

Selkirk Mts

Cranbrook

Lethbridge

Seattle

Kootenay R

Continental Divide

Spokane

Logan Pass

Kellog

Cabinet Mountains

Missouri River

MONTANA

Missoula

Big Belt Mts

Columbia River

Clarkston

Bitterroot Range

Helena

Yellowstone River

Walla Walla

Salmon River

Butte

Billings

Salmon River Mts.

Absaroka Range

Bighorn River

Bighorn Mts.

West Yellowstone

Boise

IDAHO

Snake River Plain

Shoshoni

Casper

Snake River

Pocatello

Continental Divide

Laramie Mts.

Horse C

WYOMING

Cheyenne

Great Salt Lake

Salt Lake City

Fort Collins

South Pla

Great Salt Lake Desert

Uinta Mountains

NEVADA

Denver

Colorado River

UTAH

COLORADO

Pueblo

San Juan Mts.

Virgin R

Las Vegas

Lake Mead

Santa Fe

Albuquerque

Pecos River

Continental Divide

Rio Grande River

Phoenix

NEW MEXICO

ROCKY MOUNTAIN WILDLIFE

ROCKY MOUNTAIN WILDLIFE

Text
> Don Blood

Photography
> Tom W. Hall and others

Illustrations
> Susan Im Baumgarten

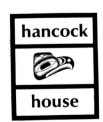
Hancock House Publishers

ISBN Cloth 0-919654-37-1
Copyright © 1976 Hancock House Publishers

Canadian Shared Cataloguing in Publication Data
Blood, Donald Arthur, 1938 -
    Rocky Mountain Wildlife

1 Wildlife watching - Rocky Mountain

I Hall, Tom W., illus. II Im Baumgarten, Susan,
illus. III Title
QL 60. B59   639
ISBN 0-919654-37-1

The artist wishes to thank Tom W. Hall and others who gave freely of their advice and photo collections to assist her in making decisions.

PRINTED AND BOUND IN CANADA by Friesen & Sons Printers.

The Publisher wishes to acknowledge the kind assistance of the Canada Council in supporting this project.

Hancock House Publishers, Ltd.
3215 Island View Road, Saanichton, B.C., Canada
Seattle, Washington. Buffalo, New York.

CONTENTS

PART II

NATURAL HISTORY FOLIOS

FOREWORD

The northern Rocky Mountains described in this book extend over a vast area from British Columbia's Peace River down to the Colorado-New Mexico border in the south. Presenting scientist and amateur naturalist alike with an immense diversity in landform, climate, and vegetation, the area abounds with a wide variety of wildlife and birds.

Author Don Blood's *Rocky Mountain Wildlife* is primarily a reference work intended for readers requiring a compact, easy-to-read compendium of information on the area's ecology, its spectacular mammals and birds, their habitats, social organization, and migratory patterns.

While many photographers have contributed to this work the magnificent photographs of one man, Tom W. Hall, stand out. Not only does Tom have one of the largest collections of wildlife photographs in North America, but it was through discussions with him that this project evolved.

I would be more than remiss if I didn't draw particular attention to the hundreds of lively and beautifully informative drawings that enhance this book. These are the creations of Susan Im Baumgarten. In addition Susan collected and selected all the material; designed and coordinated the entire book. I am sure that her efforts and special approach, carefully illustrating paragraph by paragraph the text, through photograph or drawing, will greatly aid in both, your enjoyment and understanding of this fascinating book.

This book is clearly divided into two sections. The first deals with the general geography of the Rocky Mountain Region and the behaviour and ecology of each major family or group of mammals and birds in the region. Part II, the Natural History Folios, gives a succinct textual summary and an extensive visual representation of each major species of Rocky Mountain mammal. The emphasis here is to show the life habits through photography. The two sections combined, present both a lively, informative and easy to read account plus a quick reference guide to the wildlife of North America's great mountain retreat.

INTRODUCTION

What and Where

PART I

The Rocky Mountains have had a profound, humbling influence on many people from the earliest explorers and mountain men to modern tourists. They are without doubt a striking segment of the vast North American landscape. Their distant peaks once fired the imagination of Anthony Henday, Lewis and Clark, and John Palliser, then became barely surmountable barriers to transcontinental railroads and highways, to finally become a soul-restoring retreat for millions of harassed city dwellers.

Partly because so many North Americans seek out mountainous places for relaxation and enjoyment and see them as their special places, it seems worthwhile to present a factual, illustrated account of the wild mammals and birds likely to be encountered there. Certainly the opportunity to see wildlife in a natural setting is a strong attraction for many Rocky Mountain visitors be they family campers, keen naturalists, or big game hunters.

While the term "Rocky Mountains" conjures up an instant picture in the minds of nearly everyone, the geographical extent of the Rocky Mountain region is not easy to define. Generally speaking this up and down real estate extends from the Yukon and Northwest Territories to Mexico. The eastern side of the main Rocky Mountain chain, where the Great Plains roll like a blanket to their very foot, is quite well defined. Usually a narrow band of foot-hills and occasionally an outlier of low mountains in the adjacent plains is all that separates these two great regions. To the west, however, a complex array of north-south ranges and associated intermountain basins and plateaus extend to the Pacific shores. This whole area, known as a cordilera, has a certain uniformity of wildlife due to its terrain.

But the Rockies, of all our western mountains, are best known and best loved. They have had much publicity for over a hundred years largely due to the scenic splendor of places like Banff, Glacier, and Yellowstone National Parks. Our treatment of the wildlife of this spectacular region will include typical species found in the main chain of the Rockies from about the Peace River in British Columbia to the Colorado-New Mexico border. Included are the more prominent foothills along the eastern side, and those main ranges to the west which lie between the Interior Plateau, Great Basin region and the Rockies proper. For our purposes then, the "Rockies" will include the Cariboo, Purcell and Selkirk Ranges in British Columbia, the Clearwater and Salmon River Ranges in Idaho, Uinta Mountains of northeastern Utah, and virtually all the mountains of Alberta, Montana, Wyoming and Colorado.

Incomparable Diversity

Mountain goats flourish from river bottoms to alpine crags

The great drawing card of the mountains in general and the Rockies in particular is their immense diversity in landforms and living things. No other physiographic region of North America compares with its variety of wildlife. Let's take a look at the reasons for this.

In the first place, the fauna is varied because a diversity of habitats is available; the habitats are many because of physical diversity. The physical stage on which the native plants and animals act our their life roles has been raised and twisted so that elevations, steepness of slope, and the directions which slopes face, are continually different. Superimposed on this contorted landscape are additional diversifying factors — varying soils (or lack of them), watercourses, temperature and wind, plus avalanches of snow.

Compare this region with other landscapes of North America! The extensive Great Plains (at least in its pristine state) was an ocean of grass interrupted only occasionally by badlands, sandhills or river valleys. One could walk for miles in the same kind of habitat. The vast boreal forest presents mile after mile of spruce forest broken occasionally by lakes, muskeg and fire scars, but has little physical or climatic diversity. Likewise the Arctic Tundra. Each of these huge areas of relatively similar soil and vegetation thus provide many fewer niches for wild birds and mammals to occupy. Yet there are few places in the mountains where the hiker can proceed for more than a mile or

Rocky Mountain bighorn sheep graze on grassland bench

two without passing through varying kinds of countryside.

Elevation chiefly affects wildlife habitat through variations in weather and climate. Within the region, elevations vary from about 3,000 to 13,000 feet above sea level, and climate ranges from almost desert in the southern valleys to arctic-alpine near the peaks. Mountain soils, mostly derived from broken rock, also vary with elevation. They tend to be well developed in the broad, lower valleys, less developed on the middle elevation forested slopes, and little more than pulverized rock or boulders on the higher peaks. Thus, severe climate and poor soils restrict growth of plants and productivity of wildlife habitat at higher elevations.

Anyone who labors up a mountain trail will recognize that slopes vary not only in their steepness, but also in their orientation. This orientation, the direction which they face, is known as "aspect" and both steepness and aspect affect local climate and the resulting array of plants and wildlife. In valleys running east and west, particularly, the mountain traveller may notice one side of the valley has vastly different plant growth than the other. In the Rocky Mountain region, southerly exposed slopes are usually quite open and covered with a scattering of trees, scrub or even grassland, while the northerly aspect has dense forest growth. This is because the slope facing north receives little or no direct sunlight, remains cool, and loses little moisture by evaporation. The opposite is true of the side which faces the sun. Because birds and mammals depend upon vegetation for most of their requirements, they are affected also by

Meandering river and its old water courses reflect evening light

3500
Meters

3000
Meters

2500
Meters

2000
Meters

1500
Meters

1000
Meters

14

North Slope

GL

ALPI

KRUMMHO

SUBALPINE

(Spruce - Alpine Fir - Lodgepole Pine)

(Douglas Fir -

FOOTHILLS

ALTITUDINAL CHANG

"TYPICAL" MOUNTAIN IN CENTRAL ROCKIES

TO ELEVATION

SUN

12,000
Feet

11,000
Feet

10,000
Feet

9000
Feet

8000
Feet

7000
Feet

6000
Feet

5000
Feet

4000
Feet

3000
Feet

AREA

South Slope

MONTANE FOREST

Pine)

PINYON-JUNIPER

GRASSLAND

VEGETATION ZONES

MAJOR VEGETATION ZONES IN RELATION

OSURE TO THE SUN

15

steepness and aspect of slopes, so that quite different assemblages of wildlife can be expected to occupy the two sides of such a valley.

Broad climatic patterns also affect the distribution of vegetation and wildlife in the Rockies. While local factors of elevation, steepness, and aspect already mentioned contribute to diversity on any one mountain, so do gradual differences in climate from north to south and east to west across the region. Since this region extends about 1,600 miles from south to north, climate at any one elevation becomes generally more severe as one proceeds northward, and so plants and animals take on more northern affinities.

Climate varies considerably from western to eastern slopes of the Rockies due to the so-called "rain shadow" effect. These mountains exert a powerful influence on the moisture laden air masses which move inland from the Pacific by deflecting them upward so that they drop most of their moisture on the western or windward side, spoiling many a mountain camping trip. The winds then push the now drier and lighter air masses over the mountain where eastern leeward slopes receive much less precipitation. As a result, rapid changes in rainfall and in vegetation occur over quite short distances in the Rockies, and a denser forest with more luxuriant undergrowth occurs on the western slope.

Although the rain-shadow effect is most pronounced in the coast-

West-facing slope more heavily treed

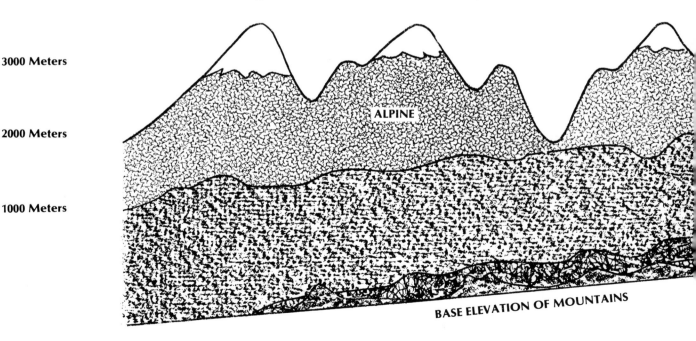

3000 Meters

2000 Meters

1000 Meters

ALPINE

BASE ELEVATION OF MOUNTAINS

LATITUDE CHANG

**CENTRAL BRITISH
COLUMBIA - ALBERTA**

al ranges — the first to be buffeted by Pacific storms — it is still noticeable in the Rockies. One of the best examples of east slope versus west slope characteristics, as well as of elevational change, will be experienced by a drive along the Going-To-The-Sun highway which completely traverses Glacier National Park, Montana.

Plants and Patterns

Despite these many complicating factors which contribute to the marvellous diversity of the Rockies, the green mantle of vegetation providing bed and breakfast for its furred and feathered inhabitants does occur in a pattern not readily observable to the casual traveller. This pattern shows up primarily as a series of elevational bands, each with its typical association of trees or other plants. Each layer of this monumental cake reaches a lower elevation as we proceed from south to north, and some of the lower ones dwindle away altogether as one approaches the Canadian border.

These elevational bands are called Life Zones, and each has been given various names by different ecologists. From top to bottom we will refer to the zones as Alpine Tundra, Subalpine Forest, Montane Forest, and Foothills. These terms will form a handy framework for later discussion about habitats occupied by characteristic kinds of wildlife.

Golden eagle with hoary marmot

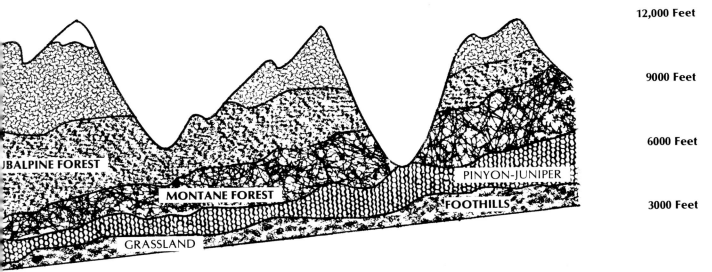

12,000 Feet

9000 Feet

6000 Feet

3000 Feet

UBALPINE FOREST

MONTANE FOREST

PINYON-JUNIPER

FOOTHILLS

GRASSLAND

VEGETATION ZONES

/EL

Stunted vegetation of alpine tundra

White-tailed ptarmigan

Hoary marmot

Alpine Tundra

The Alpine Tundra, home of ptarmigan, hoary marmot and occupied seasonally by many other species, is really an extension of the Arctic Tundra southward in the high mountains where climatic extremes are similar to the northern barrens. This zone is discontinuous, being interrupted by many broad valleys, particularly to the south. In the Canadian Rockies it is found as low as 6,000 feet, but southward its lowest elevation steadily increases about 360 feet per degree of latitude. In the central Rockies, tundra is well developed between 11,000 and 14,000 feet. The vegetation in this severe landscape is low, dwarfed and often matlike, and includes many grasses and similar plants. Even the woody plants, including willows and birch, are usually low or prostrate. Good places to explore the Alpine zone and its life include the Mount Revelstoke Summit, British Columbia; Logan Pass in Glacier Park, Montana; and Trail Ridge in Rocky Mountain National Park, Colorado.

Moving downward to the border between Alpine Tundra and Subalpine Forest, commonly called "timber line," we find either the spire-like trees of heavy snow country, or the stunted, dwarfed form known by botanists as "Krummholz." This dwarfing is largely a result of wind action. Near timber line a few hardy trees are found which neither survive in the tundra above nor compete with more dominant trees below. Bristle cone pine fills this "niche" in the southern Rockies, limber pine in the central Rockies, and whitebark pine and alpine larch in the north.

Bighorn rams summer in high country

Stunted spruce and pine grow in lower alpine meadows

Mountain goat nanny and kid graze short but nutritive alpine vegetation

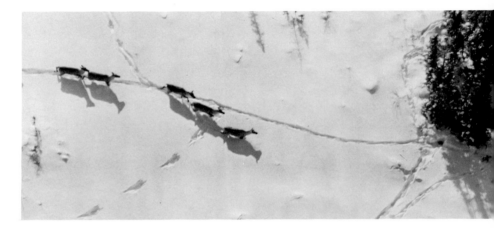

Lynx

Subalpine Forest

From timber line downward for about 2,000 feet, however, the Subalpine Rocky Mountain Forest is composed largely of Engelmann spruce and alpine fir, and is home for spruce grouse, snowshoe hare, and many other species of the boreal forest. In Montana and northern Idaho, mountain hemlock is often found in this zone, while spruce becomes common farther north. In many localities, forest fires have had a profound effect on subalpine forests, resulting in temporary invasion of aspen or lodgepole pine which may form very dense stands. When such burns are not too large they, too, serve to increase the variety of habitats available for wildlife.

Caribou search out spruce clumps for lichen and needles

Heavy winter snows often result in avalanches sweeping down through the Forest— opening space for new, more nutritive plant growth which supports new wildlife species

Burned over subalpine forest offers new and varied habitat

Subalpine meadow flowers

Montane forest of spruce and fir with ponderosa pine in dryer hotter areas

Montane Forest

In our downhill sojourn the next typical layer is the Montane Forest, home for mule deer and blue grouse. Immediately below the Subalpine zone the Montane Forest is usually characterized by Douglas fir, which often grows in such dense stands that associated tree species are negligible. However, in the southern Rockies white fir and blue spruce may occur in moist places, while in the northern Rockies grand fir on the west slope and white spruce on the east slope are commonly associated with Douglas fir.

Below the Douglas fir in the Montane zone is a belt in which the beautiful ponderosa pine forms fairly open stands. These trail away to scattered trees in savanna-like stands at low elevations. Because such widely spaced trees form little shade, the ground cover here becomes mostly grasses such as fescues and wheatgrass.

Elk browsing winter shoots

Montane Forest

Herd of mule deer foraging for winter browse in forest clearing

Here the Foothill zone is a mixture of grassland and both coniferous and decidious trees

24   Foothill zone where trees exist on cooler slopes   and in water collecting draws with grassland occurring in dryer areas (opposite)

Herd of elk grazing out into grassland

Columbian ground squirrel

Foothills Pinyon-Pine-Juniper-Grassland

In the southern Rockies, the Foothills zone supports an open coniferous forest of widely spaced small trees known as the pinon-juniper association. This is the lowest layer of coniferous or needle leaved trees, and it is not well defined north of the Snake River plain. Openings between the trees support grasses such as gramma, needlegrass and wheatgrass, numerous herbs and a few shrubs. In lower portions of the Foothills zone in the southern Rockies, the transition from coniferous forests of the lower slopes to the treeless plains or plateaus is sometimes marked by a scrub zone containing broad-leaved trees such as oak and mountain mahogany. This vegetation does not usually form a continuous cover, but occurs in dense clumps separated by areas of grassland or desert vegetation.

While not forming a definite zone, scattered tracts of grassland can be found almost anywhere in the Rockies south of the Athabasca Valley in Jasper Park. These grow usually at low elevations in the wider, drier valleys and along south-facing slopes where aspect and soils are suitable. In some places these are narrow fingers of the Great Plains grasslands which protrude into mountain valleys.

On your next trip to the Rockies, try guessing which zone you are in, and try learning to identify the typical trees. In many areas Park Naturalists or Rangers will be able to help. Such effort will add immeasurably to the enjoyment of your trip.

Pristine wilderness of the world's first National Park—Yellowstone

Pristine wilderness in all its glory

Unspoiled Wildlands

The mountainous west is unique, not only for its great natural diversity, but for its areas still remaining fairly intact. This is particularly true of the Rockies. Early explorers considered these mountains a barrier to be crossed to reach more productive lands on either side, rather than a place for permanent habitation. Later, the Rockies survived the consumptive era largely unscathed because of their remoteness, harsh climate, poor soils and difficulty for travel. In addition, but no less important, they survived through the wisdom of a few far-sighted conservationists who established many parks, forest reserves, wildlife refuges and wilderness areas. Yellowstone, the first and probably best loved National Park in the world, was established in 1872, and Banff, the first National Park in Canada, followed soon after in 1885. Today, a traveller passing the endless grain fields and fenced ranches of the plains or extensively logged forests of the Pacific slope can feel only that he has found wilderness, and perhaps himself, upon entering the sanctity of the Rockies.

Caribou trek
the mountain
wilderness

Luckily, then, the original habitat of most Rocky Mountain wildlife is relatively intact and, since habitat availability is the most important factor for wildlife survival, most of the original wild inhabitants also still exist. Undoubtedly, the distribution of some mammals like the wolf and grizzly has been greatly restricted, but virtually all of the species originally present can be found somewhere in the region, and most of the natural ecological relationships are still intact. The saga of life and death goes on, to be observed by all who have the interest and patience.

Fortunately, too, the Rockies are well situated for wildlife observation, particularly of big game animals, with a minimum expenditure of time and energy. Some of the reasons for this happy situation have been already mentioned: a variety of natural habitats, considerable country with semi-open vegetation that allows vision for some distance and many parks and reserves where wild species have learned to accept the presence of man rather than to flee at his first approach for fear of being shot. An important factor contributing to wildlife observability, is that most of the landscape is tilted nicely at an angle to the observer. By finding advantageous viewpoints the mountain wildlife buff can survey large areas such as avalanche slopes, rock slides, alpine meadows or scrubland from a single point. These factors added together make places like Jasper, Glacier and Yellowstone National Parks delightful and rewarding locations to find and to observe wildlife.

Wolf zeroing in

Grizzlies forage the high country

Mountain goats graze forest edge

Importance of Parks

Most wildlife observation in the Rockies is carried out in one or more of the many parks and reserves for which the region is world famous. These stretch in an almost continuous chain of scenic gems from the Willmore Wilderness Area in Northern Alberta to Rocky Mountain National Park, Colorado, and beyond, to include National, State and Provincial Parks, National Wildlife Refuges and Wildlife Areas, National Monuments and Primitive Areas, and Forest Reserves. Opportunities for wildlife observation are best in these areas specializing in wildlife preservation, for example, Creston Valley, B.C.; Red Rock Lakes and the National Bison Range in Montana; the National Elk Refuge in Wyoming; or in the fully protected National Parks which include Jasper, Banff, Yoho, Kootenay, Waterton Lakes, Glacier (Montana), Yellowstone, Grand Teton and Rocky Mountain.

The importance and uniqueness of National Parks and equivalent reserves cannot be over-emphasized. Here man, often the despoiler, seriously attempts to preserve not only the individual species of flora and fauna, but all their natural processes and relationships. Here man becomes a non-consumptive observer: looking, learning and receiving spiritual replenishment, but hopefully not altering the ecological systems to suit his own needs. As opposed to this unique relationship between man and nature in these reserves, man is greatly altering natural ecological relationships outside these areas, usually to achieve increased or more useful production from the land.

While factors like predator control, hunting, livestock competition for forage, lumbering, and mining cannot now affect wildlife and habitat inside National Parks, vastly increasing numbers of human visitors do pose a potential threat to the natural scene. Hopefully, park managers will be able to control local concentrations, prevent the trampling of sensitive alpine vegetation, and adequately dispose of garbage and sewage so that man's unique relationship with these pristine ecological systems is perpetuated.

Improving the Odds

Most Rocky Mountain visitors are enthralled by the scenic grandeur and are satisfied with their trip for this reason alone. Many, however, would like to enrich that experience by observing wildlife, but go home disappointed. A few suggestions may thus be in order.

First, if you really want to see wildlife, visit the mountains in spring. From late April until mid June many of the majestic big game animals will be found at lower elevations, waiting for mountain snow to melt before they proceed to summer ranges. Birds are in their most colorful plumage at this time and very conspicuous when they vocally declare territories and prepare for nesting. Also, conditions for observation are better before the full development of green foliage.

Second, autumn can be a profitable time for wildlife watchers, especially once the leaves have fallen. Animals begin returning to more accessible and restricted winter ranges so there is a general hubbub of activity with many mammals preparing frantically for winter or hurriedly carrying on annual mating rituals. In addition, as length of day decreases and temperatures drop, more wildlife activity will take place during daylight hours.

Should you be among the majority of people who can only visit the Rockies in July or August, then you cannot expect to see much wildlife along the main byways during the heat of the day, other than the sometimes amusing antics of *Homo Sapiens*. Try to get away from centres of human activity and to concentrate your efforts during morning and evening. Seek out partly open and park-like habitats such as where low elevation grasslands or alpine tundra merge with the forest.

And last, there is no substitute for local knowledge. Contact Park Naturalists, Rangers or other local authorities who can advise you where and when particular species are likely to be sighted.

A Borrowed Fauna

Mountain goat nanny and kid at mineral lick

Sharp-tailed grouse

Badger

Despite variety of habitats and diversity of wildlife, the Rocky Mountain Region claims few species as its very own. Most of its wildlife is shared with or borrowed from adjacent ecological regions. Even those mammals most commonly associated with the Rockies — wapiti, bighorn sheep, mountain goats and mule deer — are quite widespread. Some, like wild sheep and goats, while typically mountain mammals, occur in ranges and badlands outside of our region. The goats even reach tidewater on the Coast of British Columbia, and mule deer extend eastward into the sandhills of Saskatchewan and Nebraska.

Much Rocky Mountain fauna, then, is typically cordileran, that is, at home in the western mountains and adjacent rugged terrain, but not necessarily restricted to the Rockies. Other members of the fauna show affinities to the Arctic Tundra, Boreal Forest, or Great Plains. For example, the ptarmigan and mountain caribou have close Arctic relatives. Snowshoe hares, lynx, moose, and spruce grouse, typical of the Boreal Forest, extend southward in the Rockies to dwell in the Subalpine Forest zone which provides northwoods habitat as far south as New Mexico. Great plains inhabitants like the sharptail grouse, meadowlark and badger extend into the mountains where tongues of suitable grassland and scrub habitat protrude from adjacent prairies or plateaus. Special places, like marshes, are seasonal homes to a myriad of species, such as birds from the plains.

The reader should beware of trying to assign specific kinds of wildlife to particular elevations zones. Many authors refer to Alpine species or Subalpine species. But, where some species are largely restricted to a particular zone, many more are not, so it is dangerous to generalize. Birds and the larger mammals are particularly mobile and often find their seasonal requirements by utilizing several zones.

Moose and calf

MOUNTAIN MAMMALS

Mention of Rocky Mountain Wildlife usually brings to mind some of North America's most spectacular mammals. Sought with gun and camera by outdoorsmen the world over for more than 100 years, these include bighorn sheep, wapiti and grizzly bears. But the group called mammals, characterized by being warmblooded, having a covering of hair and possessing mammary glands to suckle the young, is much more diverse than this. Nearly 100 species occur in our Rocky Mountain region, varying in size from the diminutive pygmy shrew which weighs a few grams, to the wapiti and moose which may exceed 1,000 pounds.

This fascinating group is as diverse in its habits as in its size. Plant eaters, meat eaters and insect eaters, whether social or solitary, hibernaters or migrators, they have colonized the Alpine barrens, forests, rockslides and waters. They have mastered flight, life in the forest canopy, and life below the ground surface, and have adapted to sub-zero cold, desert heat and drought. Such an adaptable group is worth searching out in its Montane haunts. To make this activity more rewarding, some of the more outstanding features of species likely to be encountered by Rocky Mountain visitors are described in the following sections. We have not attempted a complete species by species account, nor arranged the treatment in the zoologist's usual systematic order. Many of the smaller mammals are secretive and nocturnal. They will be encountered seldom and thus will receive relatively less attention. Most discussion will attempt to bring out a few interesting habits, ecological relationships and adaptations of the common and typical species. Hopefully, this can make your next trip into the Rockies more satisfying, or, upon returning home, provide you with some answers to nature's puzzles encountered among crag and canyon.

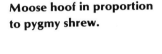

Moose hoof in proportion to pygmy shrew.

Hooves and Horns: The Ungulates

Of the eleven cloven-hoofed mammal species, known scientifically as "ungulates" occurring in North America, only the musk oxen is not found in or among the western mountains. One other, the thinhorn sheep (dall and stone sheep group) lives north of the region we are considering. Of the nine remaining species, bighorn sheep, mountain goat, caribou, moose, wapiti and mule deer may be considered typical of the Rockies, while white-tailed deer, pronghorn antelope and bison are found only in some of the more prominent valleys.

33

Caribou above treeline

AN HISTORICAL PERSPECTIVE

The species of ungulates vary greatly in their distribution patterns and abundance in the Rocky Mountain region. To understand this better, let's take a brief look at some historical factors, beginning with the most restricted species. The mountain caribou, a close relative of both the barrenground and woodland varieties, does not seem to have been abundant in the Rockies within historic times. It is seldom mentioned in the journals of the early explorers. Since then, however, this race of caribou is on the decline from long term climatic changes which have reduced its favored mature Subalpine Forest and Alpine zone ranges, and from recent habitat disturbances such as logging and forest fires on non-protected lands. Only a few remnant herds exist today. In the main chain of the Rockies, none are presently found south of Jasper National Park. Favorite haunts for them there include the high country around Maligne Lake and the Tonquin Valley. Remnant herds also occur in the Cariboo, Selkirk, Purcell and Monashee ranges in British Columbia, and one small herd extends into extreme northern Idaho in the Selkirks. Another small group is sighted frequently during winter along the British Columbia highway, near the summit between Salmo and Creston.

Caribou

Pronghorn antelope

Other species of restricted occurrence in this region are pronghorn antelope and bison. An inhabitant of the plains from Canada to Mexico, the pronghorn was estimated to range 35 million strong when Lewis and Clark saw them in 1805, but within a hundred years the population decimated to 20,000 and extinction was predicted. Protection and modern wildlife management have built up herds to about 400,000. Some of these animals enter our region in the high sagebrush-grassland valleys from southern Montana southward, where they range sporadically on both sides of the Continental Divide. Small herds can be seen at the National Bison Range in Montana, and in northern Yellowstone Park.

Buffalo

Free-ranging bison are even more restricted in this region, but their historical demise is well known and will not be recounted here. The only such herd in the Rockies occurs in Yellowstone National Park where about 700 of the shaggy beasts currently roam. The Lamar Valley is a good place to view them.

Neither numbers nor distribution of the long haired, white mountain goat seem to have changed appreciably since the time of white settlement. The habitat of this crag dweller — distributed from southern Alaska, Yukon and Northwest Territories into Montana, Idaho and Washington — has been largely immune to the ravages of man; however, certain local populations have been reduced by hunting. Their southern limit seems about the Snake River plain, although successful introductions have been made in Oregon, Colorado and the Black Hills. Goats tend to

Rocky mountain goats

35

Bighorn sheep

Elk or wapiti

be "spotty" in occurrence and some local help may be needed to find them. Good places to start are around Athabasca falls in Jasper Park, Mount Wardle in Kootenay Park and around Sperry Glacier or Mount Brown in Glacier Park, Montana.

Of the four breeds of the magnificent bighorn sheep, only the Rocky Mountain variety will concern us because its distribution falls neatly into the region we are considering. Population levels are undoubtedly much lower now than in pristine times due to loss of habitat, forage competition by livestock and diseases acquired from domestic sheep. In areas receiving total protection, however, such as in National Parks, numbers are little changed from primitive times. Sheep can be observed in many localities, particularly in Jasper, Banff, Waterton Lakes, Glacier, Yellowstone, Grand Teton and Rocky Mountain National Parks.

The Rocky Mountain species of North American elk — preferably called wapiti to avoid confusion with European moose called elk — also falls conveniently within our region. Numbers have varied historically, controlled by the occasional severe winter. Wapiti are widely distributed from northern British Columbia and Alberta to southern Colorado, but herds in the Yellowstone and Jackson Hole areas of Wyoming are probably best known.

The big-eared mule deer, the most abundant and widespread big game animal in western North America occurs in abundance throughout the Rockies, usually in the drier forests at middle and lower elevations, though it can be encountered almost anywhere. Its relative, the white-tail, prefers deciduous forest along rivers and so is found only in river valleys through fringes of the Rockies. This species is actively expanding its range northward and has replaced the mule deer in many parts of the northern Great Plains. White-tails, however, are unlikely to expand into the rugged mountains so well suited to mule deer.

Mule deer buck

White-tail buck

36

LIVING TOGETHER

Throughout much of the Rocky Mountain Region, several types of hooved mammals do occur more or less together. Since their distribution ranges overlap, and since they all eat vegetation, the reader might logically ask: How do these mammals get along together without competing with each other for food?

The answer is related to the concept of the ecological "niche." The niche of an animal includes its habitat, its food and its relationships with other species. The niche that a species occupies depends on its structural and physiological adaptations and on its behavior patterns. A basic rule of ecology is that the same niche cannot be occupied by more than one species or, conversely, that two or more species with closely similar niche requirements cannot exist indefinitely in the same area. So it is with mountain ungulates. The major advantage of one's very own niche, of course, is the escape from continuous, intense competition. Segregation into niches avoids confusion of activities between organisms, and allows each species a more efficient and orderly life cycle.

Mountain goats, bighorn sheep, mule deer, moose and wapiti all occur commonly in the northern Rockies. Each has a fairly distinct niche. The goats are associated with rugged, rocky terrain, and are found predominantly in the Alpine zone in both summer and winter. Because of the ruggedness of their habitat, the other ungulates are scarcely able to use it. Mountain sheep will usually be found on steep grassy slopes in the Alpine,

Mountain goat

Mountain goat

Bighorn sheep

Bighorn ram

37

Moose browsing

Bull elk being tranquilized so it can be moved to new range

Bull elk grazing

Long legged moose is well suited to deep snow

Subalpine, or Montane zones, but never far from rugged "escape" terrain. They graze predominantly on grasses and similar plants. Moose and mule deer are primarily forest dwellers, and feed on woody twigs known as "browse," thus avoiding competition with sheep and goats. Since moose mainly occupy shrubby meadows, bogs, edges of lakes, and burned over forest in the Subalpine zone, and mule deer prefer the Montane and Foothills zones, they largely avoid competition with each other despite similar food habitats. Moose can stay at higher elevations during winter because they are better able to cope with deep snow.

The niche of the wapiti, is, however, something of an enigma. Wapiti have a wide range of food habits (although they seem primarily browsers in the mountains) and they use many kinds of habitat. An appropriate description might be that they are "parkland" animals, preferring the semi-open meadows and avalanche slopes at the upper fringe of the forest in summer, and the aspen groves and intervening meadows at lower elevations in winter. They do venture on to the grassy slopes used by bighorns, into the shrub meadows used by moose, and open forests used by mule deer. Thus they compete for food with the other species, but do not completely usurp the niche of any.

Because wapiti numbers have increased greatly in the Rockies in the past 50 years, and because the species have over-utilized some critical winter ranges and aggressively competed with bighorn sheep, it has been labelled the "bad guy" of the Rockies by some people. Thousands of wapiti were removed from several of the National Parks by live trapping or by shooting during the past 30 years to reduce their adverse influences. In hindsight, it does not appear that this management has accomplished much of a positive nature. Wholesale reduction of wapiti numbers has now largely ceased with the realization that population levels have stabilized, and that natural competition will not result in complete decimation of other species.

It should be noted that competition by Rocky Mountain game animals for available food is likely more severe in winter than in summer. Because of the severe winter climate in this region, the area of range and availability of food is much less in winter than in summer. In summer, the mountain hiker may notice an occasional elk, moose, mule deer, bighorn and goat using the same lush meadows where Forest and Alpine zone merge. There may seem to be no segregation into niches. However, the total number of these animals in the mountains is primarily determined by the amount of suitable *winter* range, so total numbers are much lower than could be supported in summer. Thus, segregation into different habitats is less important in summer because food is super-abundant. In the winter, however, any overlap in ranges or kind of food eaten becomes a serious situation.

Deer fighting heavy snow

SURVIVING IN SNOW

Snow is a critical factor in northern and mountain environments — a factor with which all resident species must cope. Snow may reach many feet in depth at higher elevations and lie on the ground for much of the year. It covers food and is an impediment to travel, sapping the declining energy reserves of many animals while winter progresses.

One way to cope with snow is to avoid it. Many ungulates try doing so. Mountain goats choose high, steep, wind-swept slopes from which most of the snow is blown free or slides away in avalanches. Bighorn sheep retreat to lower, wind-blown slopes, where snowfall is less and orientation toward the sun most favorable. But most mountain ungulates are forced to get around and find food in a certain amount of snow, and most show varying abilities to do this.

Mountain goats picking vegetation on exposed and windblown ledges

Recently, scientists have concentrated on measuring two characteristics of game animals that affect their ability to move about in snow. One of these is the height of the animals' chest above the ground. When snow is sufficiently deep so that ungulates drag their bellies in it, they have to travel by ploughing or bounding, resulting in much loss of energy or, more likely, death due to malnutrition. High mountain areas where such deep snows are frequent are not generally inhabited by the hooved mammals in winter. Thus, the "chest height" measurement (or length of legs) indicates the ability of various species to cope with different depths of snow.

Bighorn sheep fighting snow

Wide splayed hoof of Caribou is better adapted to walking on top of snow than narrower hoofed moose

Another measurement, "track loading," is useful for judging the relative adaptation of species to varied hardness and density of snow. This measurement is calculated by dividing the weight of the animal by the total area of its four feet. If the hardness of snow consistently exceeds the track loading, or if snow is dense, animals either walk on top of it or at least sink into it for only a fraction of its total depth. Thus game animals with the longest legs (to walk in deep, soft snow) and largest hooves in relation to body weight (to walk on top of dense snow) are best adapted for survival in "snow country."

Measurements have shown that chest height of our Rocky Mountain hooved mammals decreases in the following order: moose, wapiti, caribou, bison, deer, bighorn sheep. Caribou are lightest on their feet, followed by bighorns, deer, moose, elk and bison. Among mountain ungulates, the best combination of physical characteristics to cope with snow is possessed, undoubtedly, by the mountain caribou. The moose takes second place. Bison are poorly adapted to snow, and other species are intermediate. Information is not available for the mountain goat, but neither its leg length nor hoof size seem well adapted to snow. In general, the ungulates are considered to be in difficulty when snow depth reaches two thirds of their chest height.

Deer in too deep for safety

Sheep foraging windblown slope   **Wapiti**

Then, too, factors other than physical or structural can be important for survival in snow — particularly behavior patterns for finding food, conserving energy, or avoiding extreme snow conditions. The mountain goat survives for example, in an extremely snowy, hostile environment by seeking out localized habitats which are largely free of snow through wind action and steepness. Most ungulates use their hooves to dig through snow cover to find food underneath. For this the caribou is particularly well adapted. Another approach is to feed on plant species which protrude above the snow. This is particularly evident with moose and deer. The shaggy bison has a slightly different approach. He clears away shallow snow from his grassland range with a swinging motion of his massive head and only occasionally paws the snow with his forehooves.

Caribou and buffalo digging for food

MOUNTAIN MIGRATION

Most mountain ungulates undertake some kind of elevational migration, usually in response to weather and climate. They are large, mobile animals, and thus illustrate best the phenomenon of season migrations in the Rockies. Deep and prolonged winter snows at the higher elevations are undoubtedly the most important contributing factor. Consequently, the most typical pattern becomes a forced downward movement in fall, and a voluntary upward movement in spring.

There are, however, some interesting variations in extent and timing which are superimposed on this general pattern. In the case of mountain sheep, the accepted concept of two major movements a year, one to the wintering area and one to the summer range, is only partly true. First, it is best to think of bighorn migrations as movements to and from seasonally occupied "home ranges." The home range, a much-studied aspect of mammal behavior, is considered to be the area to which an animal confines itself in its day-to-day activities. For many mammals this is one continuous area within which all the daily and seasonal requirements of food, water, protection, breeding, etc. can be found. Where migrating species have traditional summer and winter ranges, the home range is shaped essentially like a dumb bell.

Detailed studies of bighorn sheep, however, have shown an even more complex pattern. Researchers have documented five major periods in the year when Rocky Mountain bighorns move long distances to occupy seasonal home ranges. In late September and early October the rams and ewes descend to main winter ranges. Then in late October and early November the rams move to their rutting grounds, which are often not the same as their main wintering range. During late December and early January the rams usually move from their rutting grounds to different winter ranges. In late March and April, both ram and ewe groups commonly shift to late winter and spring home

Bighorn ram and lamb

BIGHORN SHEEP ALTITUDINAL MOVEMENTS

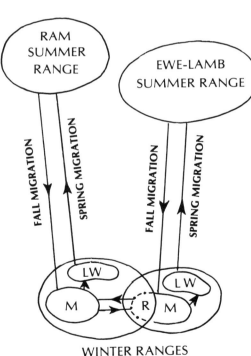

WINTER RANGES

M=MAIN WINTER RANGE
LW=LATE WINTER-EARLY SPRING RANGE
R=RUTTING AREA

Bighorn rams in pre-rutting season.

41

Bighorn ewes and lambs on winter range

ranges. Finally, at times varying from May until early July, there is traditional migration to the higher elevation summer ranges. Ram and ewe groups usually occupy separate summer ranges. Depending upon locality in the Rockies and timing of the snow melt, ewes may give birth to lambs on the winter range then undertake late upward migration. Or, if conditions consistently allow for an early upward movement, lambing will take place on the summer range.

Bighorn lamb

Summer range

The mountain caribou also have been known to undertake an intriguing departure from the accepted winter-summer range pattern, a useful change in terms of their ecological requirements. These animals perform two complete elevational migrations every year. In Wells Gray Provincial Park, British Columbia, for example, the caribou utilize Alpine meadows and the upper fringes of Subalpine forests throughout summer and early fall. During October and November they make the expected downward migration when snow covers their low growing food in the higher slopes. Eventually, the deep soft snows of early winter

Caribou with antlers in velvet

also cover much of the valley bottom vegetation and impedes free movement in search of new feeding areas. At this time the caribou turn to feeding on the lichens which hang from trees ("arboreal" lichens, often incorrectly called moss). But these are of limited quantity in the valleys. The winter picture for caribou would thus turn out to be dismal were it not that about January and February the snow usually settles and becomes more compacted. This allows these large-hooved wanderers to migrate upward on top of the snow and feed on arboreal lichens which are more abundant in the Subalpine spruce-fir forest near timberline. Here, on top of many feet of snow, the caribou are able to reach a dinner table which is far out of reach in summer. They feed almost exclusively on these tree lichens until April, when the first signs of spring appear in the low valleys, and then migrate back to the valley floor to take advantage of the earliest ground vegetation appearing through melting snow. Researchers in Wells Gray Park have noted how the spring appearance of caribou in the lowlands often coincides with the return of first crows, robins and flickers. The caribou remain in the valleys into June, grazing mainly in meadows and open forest where snow has melted most rapidly. In that month they start their standard upward migration, following spring up the Montane slopes until reaching Alpine summer pastures.

Caribou

Migrating patterns of wapiti in the Yellowstone to Jackson Hole region of Wyoming have been studied extensively by scientists, and so are probably among the best known of any big game movements. Here the migration is basically the traditional summer range to winter range and return movement. Wapiti usually arrive on the winter range of rolling, grassy valleys in November and, depending on the severity of the winter, remain through April or May. The summer ranges in Yellowstone consist of

Wapiti winter range

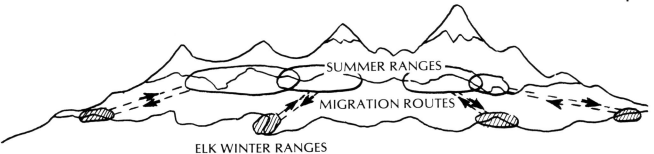

SUMMER RANGES

MIGRATION ROUTES

ELK WINTER RANGES

ELK MIGRATION PATTERNS

Biologist marking wapiti to facilitate determining migration movements

coniferous forest parkland near timberline where clearings are glades, valley and Alpine meadows, open hillsides and ridgetops. Biologists there marked an incredible total of over 1,400 wapiti with individually identifiable neck collars, and then diligently followed their movements.

This study, combined with previous ones, showed that wapiti from six distinct wintering herds spend the summer in Yellowstone. Two of these herds also winter in the park, but four other groups — the Gallatin herd of Montana, the Sunlight Basin-Crandell Creek herd of Wyoming, the Shoshone herd of Wyoming, and the Jackson Hole herd of Wyoming — spend the winter varying distances from the park. Generally, animals from each wintering herd have distinct summer ranges in the park. Although there is some mixing, individuals almost invariably return each fall to their traditional winter range. Regular migratory movements vary in airline distance from four or five miles to 50 miles or more. About 4,000 wapiti from the National Elk Refuge at Jackson Hole regularly summer in the southern part of Yellowstone, a straight-line distance of at least 50 miles. Thus the wapiti, of all resident mountain mammals, probably hold the distance record for seasonal migration. As we might expect from this versatile animal, however, it is not prone to be consistent.

Wapiti crossing river

The Wyoming studies also showed that, on occasion, a collared wapiti from the northern herd intermingled with the Jackson Hole herd on the summer ranges, then accompanied that herd south for the winter. Such animals, wintering in the Jackson Hole Valley, would be about 100 airline miles from the Lamar Valley where they had been tagged.

Wapiti on winter range

Neither are other wapiti to be labelled consistent migrators. The Madison Drainage Herd in Yellowstone is essentially non-migratory, and spends the winter at elevations in excess of 7,000 feet where average snow depth often exceeds four feet. This unusual feat is largely possible by the presence of thermal springs in and around where the animals can feed on aquatic and semi-aquatic plants through winter. They are able to move from spring to spring by using warmwater streams as travel lanes. Using such a restricted niche again points out the remarkable adaptability of the wapiti.

Wapiti herd

All of the mountain ungulates show degrees of seasonal migratory behavior, but the three just discussed probably serve well enough to illustrate the kind, variety, and extent of movements. Seasonal migrations of mule deer, moose and mountain goats also have been documented in several studies, but they are usually not so dramatic nor observable as in the case of bighorn sheep, mountain caribou and wapiti.

Wapiti

Mule deer

SOCIAL ORGANIZATION

Upon observing different species of game animals in the mountains one will probably notice that some, such as bighorns, bison, antelope and wapiti, tend to occur in groups, while others like moose and deer are more often seen singly or in pairs. The tendency of animals to associate in groups with a fairly permanent affinity for one another is referred to as sociality. What the occasional observer of these animals may not notice, however, is that sociality — particularly social structure or the sex and age composition of groups — may change seasonally.

Buffalo

There are a few aspects of social behavior in our mountain ungulates which are generally common to all species. While group size may vary, there are two basic kinds of groups: adult females with young of both sexes, and adult males. These usually mix only during the breeding season, and remain separate on sometimes widely scattered ranges during the remainder of the year. Female or matriarchal groups are usually much larger than the bachelor groups. Lastly, a well defined peck order or dominance hierarchy is usually present in any quite continuous social grouping.

Group of mountain goat nannies and kids

Bighorn rams

Mountain goat lamb

Studies of bison, a very social species, in and near Yellowstone National Park, show that bull groups are usually small clusters of one to twelve animals (average of three to four mostly four years old or older; cow groups average twenty-three members in the non-breeding season, greatly increasing in number during the rut of July and August when bull groups mingle with the cows

Herd of buffalo

Buffalo

and younger animals. As is common in the more social species, the young males stay in the cow groups until about three years of age, at which time they become mature enough to be accepted into the adult bull groups, though at the bottom of the social ladder. The social relationship of the bison bulls and cows during the breeding season has been termed a tending bond, and typically consists of one bull (usually six to eighteen years old) and one cow, although more than one such bond can be active in one group of bison at the same time. The tending bond lasts for no more than a few days, usually much less. Among bison it may be said, therefore, there is a temporary monogamous mateship. Some bulls are promiscuous, however, since they may successively mate with several cows during the breeding season. The popular belief that lone bulls are social outcasts from the herd is probably not true as these animals circulate freely during the rut. Rather like some people, they seem to prefer a solitary existence.

Bull buffalo

The general pattern of social organization and seasonal change is much the same for bighorn sheep and wapiti, but varies slightly during the autumn breeding period. In sheep society, ram groups commonly stay together near the ewe groups and individuals do not form a lasting tending bond with ewes not in heat. Once an ewe shows signs of coming into heat, however, all nearby rams show a great deal of interest, but actual mating is usually accomplished only by a dominant, large-horned ram capable of fending off his persistent but subordinate rivals. In the case of wapiti, dominant adult bulls defend a harem of cows from other bulls, and try to hold the group together to be assured of the opportunity for breeding any and all of the cows coming into heat.

Bighorn sheep mating

Elk harem

Bull elk in combat

Bull elk with harem.

Bull elk bugling

Cow moose and calf

The popular conception of a large dominant stag or bull having full control over his harem and even leading it about must be discounted as a myth. During the rut, usually the only time of the year when adult males and females associate, the female groups generally go their own way under the leadership of an older female; therefore they are not controlled by the sexually excited males who must tag along if they wish to successfully sire any offspring.

Social organization of deer and moose is more simple. The only stable social relationship is between mother and offspring, and this normally lasts only for a year until this yearling is driven away to fend for itself. In these species adult males tend to be more gregarious than females, but still the groups are usually small and temporary. During the rutting period, lone adult males wander about forest and valley searching for individual females with which to mate. The reproductive bond is short-lived in these polygamous species.

Cow moose being pestered by large twin calves trying to nurse

Bull moose

Wintering herd of bull moose

Cow buffalo and calf

In the more sociable species such as sheep, wapiti and bison, one-year-old offspring may be temporarily abandoned by the mother while she gives birth to her new young. They are not permanently driven away, but remain a part of the social group to which the mother returns with her new young. In this way, social groups develop which contain a long line of related individuals, and many traditions such as feeding areas and migration routes are learned and passed from generation to generation. Such stable social environment has survival advantages for certain species, particularly for those living in "open country" habitats which also are stable. On the other hand, it would not be advantageous for forest dwelling deer and moose to associate in social groups of herds. There is additional survival value for these animals to disperse into newly created habitats such as burned-over forest. This dispersal is mostly accomplished by yearling animals which are driven away by their elders and must search about for a suitable home range of their own.

Bison herd

Lastly, the observer of mountain mammals should note that not all aggregations have a social basis. Animals which tolerate each other may be temporarily drawn together by environmental factors such as local food abundance or salt licks, and so form large groups. These groups, however, as well as being temporary, will lack the leadership, peck order, and family relationships of truly social groups.

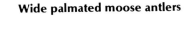
Wide palmated moose antlers

HORNS AND ANTLERS

The differences between horns and antlers, and their usefulness, for our mountain game animals has been a subject of much interest and historical debate. First, antlers are found in the deer family (wapiti, caribou, moose, mule deer and white-tailed deer) and are shed each year in winter or spring. Many people call antlers horns, but this term is incorrect. Antlers adorn only males (except in the case of caribou in which females are antlered

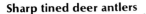
Sharp tined deer antlers

Curled horns of bighorn sheep

Sharp pointed horns of mountain goat

also). Horns, on the other hand, are permanent fixtures which normally grow throughout life and are possessed by both sexes in the family Bovidae (bighorn sheep, bison, mountain goat, and many other species). Horns of males are usually much larger than those of females. The American pronghorn antelope (which is not closely related to the true antelopes of Africa and belongs to a family all its own) shows an interesting departure. Although it grows horns rather than antlers, the outer sheath of the horn is shed each autumn but the bony core remains intact.

Semi-forked horns of pronghorn antelope . . . horny sheath is shed but bony core remains

Most people mistakenly believe the prime purpose of horns and antlers to be defensive weapons. Recent research, however, suggests that while these magnificent adornments may have evolved originally for defense, they now serve a much more important role. After all, the horns of female mountain sheep and bison are not well suited to protect the offspring from predators (goats are a different matter) and the deer family

Bighorn ewe has much reduced horns

antlers are shed in winter when needed most, while much of the rest of the year they are soft, velvet-covered tissue of little use for defense. Also, the females of the deer family, which might be expected to need antlers for defense of young, must resort either to attack with the front hooves (very effective in the case of moose) or to headlong flight.

Elk using front legs for fighting

Mule deer doe is antlerless

Mule deer in velvet

Bighorn rams

Horns and antlers are believed to serve primarily as visual insignias of rank or social status, thus indicating the relative position of each individual in the dominance hierarchy or peck order. Usually, males of the same species recognize the rank of each other based on a combination of physical factors including body size, but in species like bighorn sheep the horn size is of greatest importance.

The behavior of many mammals and some mountain ungulates in particular, is highly ritualized. There are many displays, threats and much parading about, but little actual fighting. This tends to reduce wasteful fighting which results in injury or death, expenditure of valuable energy which is hard to replenish, and susceptibility to predation. When fights between aggressive males do occur, they too are highly ritualized and designed to settle on a winner without serious injury or death. Studies show that animals with markedly different sized horns or antlers recog-

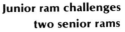

Bighorn rams displaying . . .

about to bash heads

Junior ram challenges
two senior rams

Elk in combat

Moose . . . a not too serious encounter

nize their social relationship and seldom fight. Closely matched animals, however, may require an encounter to determine which is dominant, especially if a fight confers the right to breed with a receptive female.

Serious aggressive encounters between wild ungulates usually occur only during the breeding season, and usually involve quite evenly matched individuals. Different species handle these encounters in different ways. The deer family usually lock their antlers together and engage in a great deal of shoving back and forth with appropriate snorting and groaning. They could seriously gore one another with antlers sharp at this time of the year, but they do not. This is one of the rules of cervid society.

Bighorn sheep also engage in head-to-head encounters, but accomplish this by backing off and ramming one another with considerable force and a loud report. Two large, evenly matched rams fighting in the early winter stillness are certainly a sight not soon forgotten and a sight readily observable by visitors to Rocky Mountain bighorn ranges in November and December. Although these battles may continue for several hours and result in considerable exhaustion, injury is uncommon. Evolution has provided for this. Sheep and other horned grazers which settle their disputes by head-banging are endowed with a double layer of bone on the roof of the skull, protecting them from brain damage.

Bighorn rams—a header—full force

Cross section through skull of old bighorn ram shows thickening of skull and customary hollows to absorb impact of hitting heads together

Mountain goats, both nannies and billies, carry sharp, black spike-like horns capable of inflicting mortal wounds. Horns of the billies are slightly larger than those of the nannies. Consequently, goats have evolved intense threat displays and have reduced fighting to a minimum. Studies show that when goats do fight they use a different technique than most other hooved mammals. They fight not head-to-head, but side by side while moving about one another. Goats strike up and sideways with the head, the horn blows landing mainly on the chest, front legs and belly. Since the sharp horns hit point first, such fights, while rare, are extremely damaging. As a result, injury and death from fighting seem more common among goats than other ungulates.

Mountain goat nanny with young

Mountain goat

Mountain goat horns are deadly weapons rarely used

Mountain goat, threat position

Mountain goat

Bighorn ram

Mule deer with antlers in velvet

Evolution, however, also served the goat well. Goats have a very thick, tough hide, which Indians of the Alaska coast recognized for its worth and used as breast armour. This hide is particularly well developed around the hind quarters where blows are most often received. But to reduce the necessity for fighting, evolution favored the survival of goats which "display" rather than fight, and which show inhibition toward striking others. Interestingly enough, this results in a unique social system where the animals most capable of doing damage, adult billies, are least likely to fight and are subordinate to both females and yearlings.

The role of horns and antlers in the life of many species is still imperfectly known. But the reader, hopefully, upon encountering these ponderous adornments while afield, will now have some understanding of their social importance.

As mentioned earlier, horns are permanent fixtures which adorn both sexes and grow throughout life. In bighorn sheep, horn growth occurs in summer and ceases each winter, resulting in a growth ring which is a convenient method of determining age. Care must be taken, however, not to confuse the annual growth rings with other, less distinct, "false annuli". Most horn growth occurs during the first 3 or 4 years of life, and the distance between growth rings decreases as age increases. Horns of old rams may reach four feet in length around the curl and sixteen inches in circumference around the base. Those of adult ewes are only about a foot long, and much thinner at the base.

Antlers of the deer family are typically shed in winter or early spring, re-grown during the summer, and carried in their hardened form during the fall or early winter mating period. Except in the case of caribou, they adorn males only. Visitors to the mountains in summer are most likely to see antlers in their growth phase, when they are covered with "velvet". The furry velvet is well endowed with blood vessels, and provide nourishment for the bony antlers as they grow outward from the skull. Once the antlers have hardened, the velvet dries and is shed or rubbed off, usually during August or September.

Members of the deer family vary somewhat in the seasonal pattern of antler growth and shedding. For example, most moose antlers drop in December, and January, deer in January and February, and wapiti in March and April. Yearling males also deviate somehat from older animals, usually shedding the antlers later and carrying the velvet longer. The caribou, in both sexes are antlered, also show an interesting pattern in which antler growth is about six months out of phase between sexes. Antlers of the bulls may not be velvet-free until October, yet are dropped as early as November and December. Cow caribou carry antlers until April or May. The dropping of the female antlers is physiologically linked to the birth of the calves.

SCENTS AND SOUNDS

The ungulates are not renowned for their vocal repertoire, but do communicate by a variety of sounds, scents and visual signals.

Vocalizations are most common during the mating season. Bison bulls, for example, produce a guttural bellow which can be heard at least three miles on a calm day. Only animals three or four years of age and older produce this sound frequently during the rut and rarely at other times. A less common sound, also restricted to adult bulls during the rut, is a snort produced by a rapid expulsion of air through the nostrils. This sound will carry over one half mile in still air. Bison also produce a variety of sounds best described as grunts, and calves bawl.

Buffalo or bison bellowing

The most notable sound made by wapiti is the piercing whistle or bugle of adult bulls during the rut. A high mountain valley in elk country during September may reverberate at dusk with the spine tingling call of several rutting males, a wilderness experience never to be forgotten. For obvious reasons, many hunters have learned to imitate this call. Only bulls over two years of age are known to whistle. The whistle serves to communicate the presence of one sexually active bull to others in the area, probably as a challenge. When faced with potential danger, wapiti of both sexes, may produce an "alarm bark," a call of short duration repeated usually two or more times. When elk are separated from one another, particularly calves from cows, they frequently produce a squeal until reunited.

Bison calf

Elk bugling

Moose are known to have three or four distinct calls: an alarm call used by both sexes, a whine used by calves to attract their mothers, and a short grunt used by females to attract their young. In addition, the bulls have a low, sometimes rhythmically repeated call which they utter when courting cows, when approaching opponents, or when moving about. All species produce specific sounds, but these examples will serve to illustrate the point.

Preorbital gland of deer

The ungulates also possess a variety of scent glands in the skin, most commonly on the feet and head. For example, both mule deer and white-tailed deer have a preorbital gland in front of the eye, tarsal and metatarsal glands on the legs, and interdigital glands between the toes. Secretions from these glands serve a variety of social, communicatory functions. Secretions from well

SCENT GLANDS OF DEER

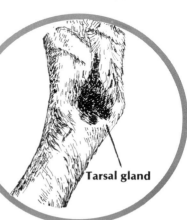
Tarsal gland

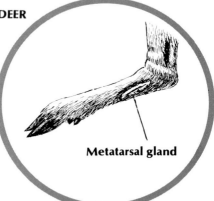
Metatarsal gland

Interdigital gland.

developed glands, for example on the head, of mountain goats and antelope are used by adult males to "mark" brush or clumps of grass and thus intimidate other males. These glands are particularly active during breeding season, when goats may be seen violently horning a variety of objects to transmit this scent to them. Scent from foot glands obviously marks the travels of its

Mountain goat

Oil gland—located at base of horn in both sexes but it is largest in the male, particularly during the rut. By rubbing and slashing bushes with his horns, a scent is left for the other goats to heed

Tracks—leave scent trail

owner, and so helps forest dwelling species retrace their tracks in strange country, locate mates during the breeding season, or advertise their presence to other deer they wish to attract or intimidate. This is important for deer because they depend on scent to a greater degree than on hearing and sight. Scents are also very important to help mothers locate their young. This applies both to fawns of the deer family hidden away in dense cover while the mothers feed, and to young bison, caribou, wapiti, or bighorn. All may be identified among a large social group by means of scent, and thus maintain contact with the correct parent. Dams of these social species apparently recognize the smell of their own young and will reject, sometimes violently, a confused youngster which tries to suckle a mother not its own.

"Flehmen" lip curl of bighorn ram

Observers of mountain ungulates, and mammals generally, often fail to recognize the profound importance of smell in the daily life of these animals, mostly because the human sense of smell is not nearly as well developed. Future research undoubtedly will show further ways in which scent is important in the social life and communication of this fascinating group.

Bull elk with harem

Bighorns scenting

In addition to sounds and smells, certain visual signals may be important for ungulate communication. Each species has an array of postures, displays and threats which transmit very definite information to other animals, usually of the same species. These are very complex and will not be described here. Other visual signals are important indicators of danger, particularly for open-country species for which the sense of sight is most important. Typical examples are the bobbing flag of the alarmed white-tailed deer, and the white rump-patch of the pronghorn antelope. The antelope has long white hairs on the rump which are suddenly raised when it is disturbed. In that state they form two large white rosettes that are visible from a great distance. These serve as an alarm signal readily recognized and responded to by other antelope in the area, bringing obvious survival advantages in situations such as predator attacks.

Whitetail deer—giving warning flash from tail as it departs

Pronghorns with inflated rump patch

Pronghorns on alert

Mountain goats

WALKERS AND RUNNERS

The rocky mountain goat has the best reputation as a mountaineer, and not without cause. Goats are walkers, running rarely even when disturbed. Headlong flight among the crags of their alpine habitat would be dangerous even for these superbly adapted animals.

At any rate, they are usually only a few fast paces from cliffs which are impassable for their enemies. Goats are square, broad animals with heavy leg muscles, flexible legs, and broad square hooves. The hooves have a horny outer shell and an inner pad of tough rubbery material which affords excellent traction on steep rocks. The outer shell is very hard and will support the animals'

Agile mountain goats

Square hooves of
mountain goat

weight even when standing on a minute foothold where a small part of the hoof surface is supported. Goats are methodical walkers, deliberately picking their way, but they also jump when necessary. In traversing difficult terrain they may bound and land once on a cliff face where they are unable to stand, then immediately bound again to a safer footing.

Mountain goats traversing difficult terrain

Mountain goats deliberately picking their way . . .

Goats are methodical walkers, deliberately picking way, but they also jump when necessary . . . as do the bighorn sheep

Bighorn sheep are good mountaineers also, but less so than goats. Sheep are better adapted to running in open terrain and use it more frequently than goats. They are also excellent jumpers.

Whitetail trot

Many different gaits have been described for hooved mammals. We do not have space here for complete details but it may be apt to quote that keen observer of nature , Theodore Roosevelt who wrote:

> ". . . there can be no question as to the infinitely superior grace and beauty of the white-tail when he either trots or runs. The mule-deer and blacktail bound . . . The prong-horn gallops with an even gait, and so does the bighorn when it happens to be caught on a flat; but the white-tail moves with an indescribable spring and buoyancy . . ."

Roosevelt did not mention the ungainly moose. Although it is not particularly adapted to mountainous terrain, this long-legged "deer" is adept at negotiating rough country. Those long legs help him travel through tangles of fallen trees (their useful-

Long-legged moose easily traverses deep snow and thick brush

Moose

ness in deep snow has already been observed) and those cloven hoofs spread widely to support him when he wades through muskeg. It is amazing that such an ungainly looking animal with antlers spreading over four feet across can negotiate thick woods in relative silence.

Of all mountain game, the moose is best adapted to water. They have been known to swim as far as twelve miles and to dive as much as eighteen feet when feeding on submerged aquatic plants. They frequently seek water as a refuge from the biting flies which are abundant in their swampy habitats during summer.

The aquatic moose

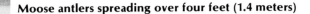

Moose dive to 18 feet for food and can swim many miles

Moose feeding on submerged aquatic plants

60

A FEW PECULIARITIES

Little oddities of behavior can make a wildlife watching trip most rewarding. Most mammals, some more than others, engage in behavior known as comfort movements. Such movements relate to body care such as grooming the pelage. Mammals use the most accessible means to accomplish this: horns, antlers, hooves, tongue or teeth.

Comfort movements have been described best for mountain sheep. Their most common movement in spring is body rubbing. They seek out boulders, trees or bushes against which to polish their sides, shoulders and hindquarters. This serves to dislodge the heavy, matted winter hair not needed in summer. Bighorns also scratch the withers with their horns, although large rams have difficulty doing so because they cannot reach their body with the horn tips. Other comfort movements involve scratching the front quarters with a hind leg or, less frequently, using the tongue and teeth for cleaning the fur.

Bighorn body rubbing

Doe using tongue and teeth . . .

buck licking · · ·

· · · scratching

Buffalo

Similar behavior has been reported for bison. Their "rubbing stones" are well known on the plains. Bison also engage in the fine art of "wallowing" in which they roll on their sides and backs in exposed, dusty soil. This seems to have a grooming function. Wallowing is carried out by both sexes of bison at all seasons, although it is most commonly practised by bulls during the breeding season. Unlike bighorns and bison, others, such as moose, wapiti and deer, normally do not rub off their moulting hair. Comfort movements have also been found to be limited in the case of mountain goats, which have the heaviest and thickest winter coat of all. Probably their coat is too thick to allow efficient grooming with hooves or teeth.

Buffalo wallowing in dust

Goat shedding winter coat

**Mountain goat
resting on rump**

White-tail deer stretching

White-tail rubbing tips of antlers

There is a solution to every biological dilemma, however, and the goats have solved theirs by taking dirt baths, primarily during June. They either lie on one side and rub back and forth, or they lie upright and paw dirt over themselves with a side arm movement of front legs. The thick underwool becomes impregnated with sand or dirt which seems to aid the shedding process. Mountain goats occasionally assume an interesting and amusing posture by sitting nonchalantly on their rumps, braced up by their front feet.

Other comfort mannerisms of most ungulates include yawning and stretching. In addition, the antler bearing species — wapiti, deer and moose — often rub the tips of their antlers under a hind leg when the antlers are in velvet. This may provide relief from itching when the antlers are growing rapidly in summer. Still other movements, such as shaking the body, jerking the legs and flipping the ears, serve to dislodge or discourage biting insects.

With regard to bedding, both mountain sheep and goats usually scratch out a suitable bed, presumably to remove uncomfortable rocks or debris. Beds are normally in exposed places with a good view of the surrounding countryside, and the animals normally lie facing downhill away from the mountain. Goat and sheep beds are usually used over and over again, probably for generations. The resulting accumulation of fecal material often results in a lush growth of grass around the margin of these beds. Unlike sheep and goats, however, members of the deer family seldom seem to bed down twice in exactly the same place.

Mountain goat day-bedding

Bighorn rams day-bedding

Elk standing upright to fight
with front hooves

Long legged browsing moose
kneeling in order to graze

Grazing mountain goat
climbing tree to browse

Diligent observation may yield no end of behavioral oddities, such as short-legged grazing goat standing upright to reach food, long-legged and short-necked browsing moose, kneeling down to graze on grass, or sparring encounters between wapiti bulls.

Fascinating interaction between the animals and their habitat may also be noted, like the wapiti signature below left on chewed aspens, or horning a defenceless sapling.

Elk horning a tree to clean antlers

The harsh 1947 winter food shortage caused many animals to chew cambium layer of trees—they still bear scars

And, like the mountain hiker about to ford a turbulent stream, our hooved friends may also procrastinate at length before taking the plunge.

BIGHORNS PROCRASTINATE AT THE CROSSING

The wait . . .   **the jump . . .**

the line-up

The Bears

A Rocky Mountain traveller who encounters a bear in his camp-ground or along a mountain trail will have no difficulty in recognizing the animal for what it is. Detailed physical descriptions are unnecessary; it is enough to say that only two kinds of bear species are found within the region; the large grizzly and the smaller black bear.

There has been much confusion in the naming of bears, both by scientists and the public, mostly because of bears' various color phases. After hearing vaguely of brown, black, and grizzly bears, kermodi bears, glacier bears, kodiak bears, plains grizzly and barren-ground grizzly, observers may be surprised to note that only three basic kinds or species exist in North-America: polar, grizzly and black. These names apply to geographical variations of grizzly and black bears, the only two species of concern here.

. . . a picnic lunch

THE BEARS

Polar   **Grizzly**   **Black**

The much maligned grizzly group, often called big brown bears, includes the large kodiak bears of coastal Alaska, smaller barren-ground (tundra) animals, and the mountain variety. Their hair color varies extremely from cream through brown to black, frequently with white tips giving a grizzled appearance.

Black bears are widely distributed through forested parts of eastern and western North America, and vary little except for color. In the Rockies, the color normally is distinctly black or distinctly brown, although in isolated areas of the Pacific coast, both white and blue phases have been described. Thus we have black colored big brown bears, and brown colored "black bears". Where grizzly bear colors are mainly variations on a theme, black bear coloring is genetically inherited. Therefore, the proportion of brown-colored black bears in the population varies from area to area. The brown phase is more common in the Rockies and adjacent Great Plains than elsewhere, while surrounding populations on the Pacific coast, Boreal Forest and Eastern Deciduous Forests are almost entirely black. In some places in the Rockies, the brown phase is more common than black. Both colors can occur in the same black bear family group, suggesting a pattern of inheritance similar to eye color in humans.

Black bears come in many color phases —black, brown, cinnamon, yellow, white, blue

Potential danger

The observer startled by an unexpected bear will not likely have the desire nor presence of mind to determine whether the intruder is a black bear or grizzly. However, for those fortunate enough to observe either from the safety of a vehicle, or from the opposite side of an alpine valley with the aid of binoculars, they will see the grizzly's main distinguishing characteristics are the large size, usually grizzled coat, prominent shoulder hump, and dish-shaped face. In contrast, the black bear is of smaller size, usually very black or very brown color with a blaze of white on the chest, lacks a shoulder hump, and has a straight or Roman

Black bear—lacking shoulder hump of ⋯   grizzly

Juvenile grizzly

nose. Size is a poor characteristic to rely on without something to judge against. Even then, juvenile grizzlies could be confused with adult blacks. The grizzly's claws are also much longer than the black's but, hopefully, most people will not get close enough to determine this!

Grizzly photographed by spotlight—note long claws

Female black with two yearling cubs

Black bears are found in good numbers throughout the Rockies. Except in the more heavily settled valleys, their tally is probably changed little from pre-settlement days. The grizzly's distribution and count, however, has greatly diminished, particularly in the Great Plains, Southern Rockies, Intermountain Region and Coastal Ranges. Fortunately, a few thrifty populations remain in the Rockies, particularly in the National Parks. About 150 to 200 grizzlies are believed to exist in and around each of Glacier and Yellowstone National Parks. Smaller numbers occur outside these parks in adjacent Montana, Idaho and Wyoming. The furthest south population of grizzlies in the United States is a remnant group in Colorado, believed to number about ten animals. Within the area defined for this book, total grizzly numbers probably run about 500 to 800 on the U.S. side of the border, and 1,500 to 2,000 on the Canadian side.

Grizzly sow and
cubs scramble up slide

ECOLOGICAL "IN-BETWEENS"

The bears fill an interesting ecological position, being neither true herbivores (plant-eaters) like the ungulates discussed previously, nor true carnivores (meat-eaters) like the cougar, wolf and many others. While bears' dentition most closely resembles true carnivores, their food habits are very broad, fitting them for the title of omnivores (everything-eaters). Feeding habits vary from place to place and with changing seasons. Since bears have proven very adept at scavenging and seeking out whatever is locally available, they may also be called opportunistic feeders.

Intensive studies of black bears in Montana, for example, show that vegetation in the form of green foliage, blossoms, seeds or berries makes up the bulk of their diet during all seasons. In general, black bear foods include about 70% to 80% plant material, 10% to 15% insects, and 10% to 15% mammals, birds and related animal material.

OMNIVORE SKULL

Black bear—back teeth flat for grinding

Cougar—back teeth sharp for cutting

CARNIVORE SKULL 67

Black eating succulent horsetails . . . and berries below

Green vegetation, becomes especially important in the spring when black bears may be seen grazing like sheep on small meadows among the forest. Main spring foods are grasses, angelica, sweet cicely, horsetail, clover, cow parsnip, dandelion blossoms and ants. Summer foods are similar, but grasses become less important and berries begin to be used. In autumn, huckleberries, blueberries and cones of the whitebark pine are preferred, but green vegetation is still important. Other significant fall foods are currants, service berries, and mountain ash berries. Insects, especially ants, are the most frequent animal

Black bear eating carrion —road killed moose

food. Remains of a variety of mammals including big game have been found in black bear droppings, but this contribution to their diet is minor and much of this food is obtained as carrion. On rare occasions black bears have been known to prey on young and even adult hooved mammals, such as elk, but normally they are only able to dispatch diseased or emaciated individuals, or newborn young separated from their mothers. Several smaller mammals including mice, chipmunks, ground squirrels, pocket gophers and porcupines are eaten occasionally.

Small black cub teething

An interesting habit of black bears of concern to foresters is that of "cambium feeding". A variety of trees serve this purpose. Trees are damaged when bears strip bark from them to expose the layer between bark and wood known scientifically as *cambium*. This nutritious layer is licked or chewed sometimes killing the tree. Cambium feeding is most common in spring and early summer when trees are most actively growing and the sap is flowing.

Carrion-eating grizzly

Grizzlies are adaptable feeders, having proven their ability to capitalize on spawning salmon, Arctic rodents, alpine vegetation, carrion and garbage. Natural populations in the Rockies, like the black bear, are largely vegetarians despite their ferocious reputation as killers of livestock, trophy game animals, and, occasionally, man.

Grizzlies at garbage dump

In areas such as Glacier National Park in the Selkirk Mountains of British Columbia, where snowfall is great, vegetation lush, and game populations sparse, the grizzly is almost entirely a vegetarian. Here plant materials such as grasses, sedges, horsetail, huckleberries, blueberries and mountain ash berries make up an estimated 98% of their diet. On the east slope of the Rockies,

Grizzly eating succulent greens

Carrion-eating grizzly

however, where game animals are more abundant, the ungulates assume greater importance in the grizzly diet. These animals are eaten largely as carrion, although being a powerful predator, the grizzly does regularly kill young or weakened big game animals in some areas. Studies of relationships between wapiti and grizzlies in the Madison River area in Yellowstone show how bears commonly scavenge on dead animals, hasten the death of wapiti predestined to die from malnutrition, prey on a portion of the newborn calves, and kill an occasional older healthy wapiti that has been chased into deep snow or was just not sufficiently wary. A related finding of interest describes how other scavengers such as coyotes, ravens and magpies very quickly consumed the carcasses of wapiti killed by grizzlies, thus forcing the bears to make more kills than needed to satisfy their own requirements. Yet such natural ecological relationships help to maintain a stable and healthy wapiti herd.

Coyotes and ravens cleaning up kill

As a result of their powerful build and long claws, grizzlies are also able to obtain more food by digging than do their smaller cousins. These foods include roots of the legume *hedysarum*, and burrowing rodents such as marmots, ground squirrels and pocket gophers.

Richardson ground squirrel

Grizzly bear digging

Seasonal habitats occupied by bears are mostly a reflection of food availability, although other factors such as cover and den sites have an influence. In general, the black bear is found in more densely forested habitat at lower elevations than the grizzly, but there is considerable overlap. Grizzlies make considerable use of Alpine meadows, openings among the upper part of the Subalpine Forest, shrubby avalanche slopes, and Alluvial flats along streams. Black bears are found more

Grizzly hunting open meadows

Curious black bear

70

Grizzly

Grizzled black bear foraging meadow

Black bear searching open woodland

commonly in the lower part of the Subalpine Forest and in the drier Montane forest and Foothills zones. The grizzly's search for food takes it normally from Subalpine Forest and avalanche slopes in spring to the Alpine zone in summer, then back to avalanche slopes and Alluvial flats in fall. Black bears also use varying habitats as seasons change, but have smaller home ranges and undertake less pronounced altitudinal movements than grizzlies. In the Rockies the black bear is found commonly in small dry forest openings and along roadsides and streambanks in spring and early summer. These are the earliest areas to "green-up" in spring. During late summer and fall they are found mostly in spruce, fir or lodgepole pine forests, taking advantage of berries and insects. Denning also takes place in the forest. Black bears make little use of avalanche slopes and wet meadows, avoiding open exposed logged-over forest areas for several years until new growth appears.

Black bear tracks

HOME RANGE AND MOVEMENTS

In the Rockies, black bears emerge from their winter dens between mid April and mid May (more about denning later) and spend the summer in familiar home ranges. In areas of diverse topography and vegetation such as the Whitefish Range in Montana, black bears numbers are high (about one per square mile) and home ranges are relatively small. Maximum daily movements of females are about one and a half miles; those of males about four miles. Maximum home range areas are about two and twelve square miles respectively. Home ranges are not defended as "territories" are, and those of adult males and females commonly overlap. Except during the breeding season, however, males and females usually observe a mutual distance of 50 yards or more. Home ranges are mutually respected by adults of the same sex; thus those of two females or two males overlap very little. This seems nature's way of ensuring enough food for all.

Black bear

Juvenile black must search out vacant home range before he is two years old

Grizzly on the move

Adult black bear

Nevertheless, longer movements may be made by juvenile black bears in search of a vacant home range, by bears habituated to garbage feeding, or by virtually any bears in cases of extreme food shortage.

Movements of grizzlies are somewhat greater than those of black bears, consequently home ranges are larger. In good habitat, female home ranges may be about 25 square miles and those of males about 100 square miles. Females with young tend to range more widely than those without young. For Yellowstone Park, two types of grizzly home ranges have been described. One is a well defined area used throughout the year. The other consists of a summer and early fall feeding area connected by a migration route to an early spring and late fall area containing the winter den. In the Park, grizzlies tagged with radio transmitters have travelled up to 30 airline miles to reach their den. Grizzlies relocated to strange habitat usually return promptly. Homing movements of up to 70 miles have been recorded.

In good grizzly habitat, population densities (including all sexes and ages) may reach one bear per ten square miles. Densities in Banff and Yellowstone Parks, however, seem about one bear per 20 or 30 square miles.

SOCIAL LIFE IN THE BEAR WORLD

The only stable social group in both black and grizzly bear society is the family group, consisting of a sow and her cubs or yearlings. This union usually persists for one and one half to two and one half years, at which time the female breeds again. Evidently, adult males (boars) disrupt the family group during the summer breeding season through aggression toward the young of their prospective mate.

The female black bear and her cubs are associated constantly during their first summer. They are weaned normally in Sept-

Black sow and cubs off to picnic area

ember, when about seven months old. They den together, closely huddled, and continue this relationship well into their second summer. Communication within the family group involves a variety of sounds. Small cubs "squall" when hungry, when uncomfortable or frightened, and "purr" when comfortable and contented. Their purr actually resembles a rapid series of low grunts. Older cubs often voice a pleading bawl to the mother. The female uses a huffing call to her cubs, and disciplines them by swatting. Females often become aggressive in defense of their young.

Black bears . . . sow drinking . . .

Black bear

cub squealing

Social life in the grizzlies is similar, except that several generation family groups are more common. Mixed age litters have been reported, and likely are a result of old offspring rejoining their mother after she has had a new litter. A case of an adult female adopting two yearling cubs of another sow has also been reported.

Family life or "care-dependency" behavior gives rise to cultural inheritance, and is well developed in bears due to the long relationship of young with the mother. Social communication is important in training and survival. An additional benefit from family behavior is heat conservation during the denning period when mother and young huddle for warmth. Survival of the young is enhanced when the family group endures longer, since other adults, usually males, will either kill unprotected young or chase them away from favorable habitat.

Sow grizzly muzzling cubs

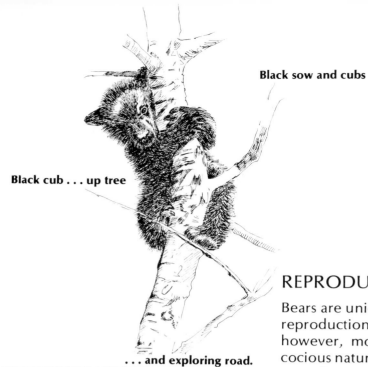

Black cub . . . up tree

. . . and exploring road.

Black sow and cubs

Black bear cubs

REPRODUCTION

Bears are unique in North America for having the lowest rate of reproduction of any land mammal. This low rate is adequate, however, mostly because of lengthy maternal care and precocious nature of the young, both of which result in low juvenile mortality.

Black bears in the Rockies breed during June and July. This is the only time when adult males and females are seen together. Females usually do not breed until four and a half years old or older, and their first attempt to raise a litter often is unsuccessful. The young are born in the winter den about February, and weigh only about half a pound. Average litter size is two, although extremes of five and six have been reported. Black bear females normally produce young every second year, but in areas where nutrition is poor, every third year may be more common.

Grizzly bears

Grizzly cubs

Grizzlies in the Rockies mate during June, and gestation is about eight months, again with cubs born in the winter dens about early February. Females do not breed for the first time until four and one half to eight and one half years of age. Young are born every two or three years — the latter interval being most common. First litters usually consist of one or two cubs, while later litters may vary from one to four. Thus the total reproductive output of a population is very low.

Grizzlies seldom live beyond 20 years in the wild, although ages of 30 to 40 years have been reported in captivity.

74

WINTER DENNING

Permanent mountain dwellers show a variety of approaches to the vicissitudes of winter. Where birds and bats may fly to sunnier climates, and ungulates migrate to lower elevations or just tough it out, bears choose to doze away the winter in protected dens. In view of the deep snows and scarcity of food in their usual haunts in winter, this course of action is wise indeed. Bears are not true hibernators, since their winter "dormancy" or "lethargy" is not characterized by the pronounced changes in bodily function found in marmots and ground squirrels. Bears are "light sleepers," easily aroused from their winter relaxation. However, their body temperature drops a few degrees during dormancy, while heart beat and breathing rate slow down considerably.

Fortunately, some excellent studies of bear denning behavior have been carried out in the Rockies. They have shown that winter dormancy is a very fundamental part of bear ecology, and that the entire annual cycle of bear activity is related to preparing for denning, denning itself, or recovery from this process.

In the central Rockies, grizzlies usually enter their dens during November, although dates depend on severity of fall weather and can vary by as much as a month. Final movement to the isolated den sites usually occurs during a snowstorm which covers the tracks — apparently a protective function. Most dens are in the upper part of the Subalpine Forest at elevations of 6,000 to 9,000 feet, and are usually oriented toward the north because the denning bears benefit from the insulation of deeper snow and less frequent melting which could result in a wet, uncomfortable den.

Grizzly dens are dug well in advance of actual "hibernation," usually in late September and October. The major excavation takes only a few days. Even though available, natural shelters are not used by grizzlies. These powerful beasts prefers to dig their own. Usually dens are dug under the roots of trees or stumps, or occasionally under logs or into hillsides. Tree roots often form a ceiling for the den, and their spacing may limit the size of the entrance. Den size is just adequate for the number of bears housed, whether an individual or a family. Females with cubs or yearlings sleep in the same den in close contact with their offspring. Some dens have long entrance tunnels, in others the entrance may open directly into the sleeping chamber. The small size of dens becomes important to retain the body heat of its inhabitants. Grizzlies assemble a bed in the den, usually of spruce or fir boughs from near the den. Occasionally grass and moss is used, probably by pregnant females desiring a softer bed for the expected young. A compact den with a deep bed and an entranceway plugged with snow is a considerably warmer environment than outside.

Grizzly eats from kill during light snowfall before denning

Grizzlies on the move

GRIZZLY BEAR DEN

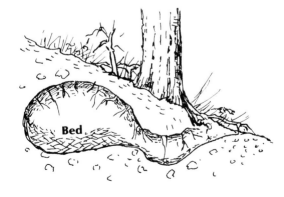

Bed

Den dug so the bed lies slightly above entrance to help trap heat and provide a relatively constant den temperature until deep snow seals entrance.

From Wildlife Monographs No. 43 1972
Frank C. Craighead, Jr. and John J. Craighead,

Grizzly

Grizzlies emerge from their dens about late March after a five month fast, although very occasionally one may emerge in mid-winter. Usually they remain and feed in the den vicinity for several weeks until the deep wet snow is melted sufficiently to allow travel with ease. Females with cubs are the last to abandon the site of their den. Dens are seldom re-used in subsequent years, and seem not to be actively defended.

Black bears apparently use a wider variety of sites for denning, usually at lower elevations, and enter their dens slightly earlier than grizzlies — about early October in the Rockies. In addition, they usually use natural cavities such as hollow trees or rock caves, although they have been known to den under cabins and in culverts, as if finding man's structures less repugnant than their grizzled relatives. Black bears form a hollow in the den in which to lie, but only some individuals, perhaps females, improve the den by bringing in bedding material. Behavior in the den includes the tendency to huddle, to curl the body, and to shiver, all of which are important in conserving or producing heat.

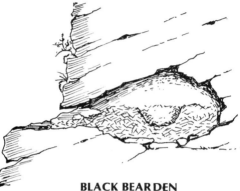

BLACK BEAR DEN
A natural cave with a bed of foliage

Denning black bears approached by human observers usually show great reluctance to leave, occasionally allowing access to within two feet. Sometimes this is true of grizzlies, also, but they seem more variable in their responses to human presence.

Grizzlies also construct "daybeds" which should not be confused with dens. These shallow excavations up to eighteen inches deep in the forest floor, usually close to feeding areas, may be used by different bears, and are not necessarily on north-facing slopes or at the base of large trees. Some daybeds are used only once, others repeatedly.

SAFETY IN BEAR COUNTRY

The bears' reputation for ferocity is almost legendary, particularly in the case of the grizzly. Unfortunately, there is an element of truth here which cannot be ignored. Most statistics on human injury or death from bear attacks have been kept by the National Parks. They reveal that the majority of injuries are attributable to black bears, but most deaths (fortunately few) are a result of grizzlies. Over the years, a total of eight deaths were attributable to bear attacks in combined National Parks of the United States and Canada.

In a relative sense, therefore, the bear hazard is slight. It has been estimated that the injury rate from grizzlies in all North American national parks inhabited by this species is one injury per two

Grizzly on prowl—photographed by spotlight

Cinnamon phase black relaxing in wrong location

million visitors, and the death rate is one per thirty million. However, this includes those visitors who merely motor through the parks, so that the hazard undoubtedly is higher for the smaller number of people who frequent the back country.

Sow black with one black cub and one cinnamon cub

Under natural conditions only one situation occurs where bears may be expected to threaten or actually attack humans. This is when a person comes too near a sow's cubs or yearlings — particularly if one blunders between mother and young. Most other cases of injury are a direct result of bear behavior which has been modified by man, for example, allowing bears access to garbage cans and dumps, to food hampers in campgrounds, or worse still, actually providing handouts at the roadside. Unfortunately, bears often bite the hand that feeds them; also, once accustomed to man's food, they will go to great lengths to obtain it. Garbage and human food is the catalyst responsible for the majority of harmful contacts between man and bears. It is lamentable that many bears, in fact, too many bears, must be destroyed every year because they have been made dangerous by well-meaning or ignorant people who have fed them.

Grizzly chases black from garbage dump

The public is generally opposed to pollution. The roadside bear, like the urban rat, is a direct result of environmental pollution. Hopefully the public is becoming aware of this fact, and the demand to see demoralized beggar bears will be replaced by a desire to see bears behaving normally in their natural habitat.

A few rules may be in order for Rocky Mountain campground users. First, never store food in one's tent or leave picnic hampers and coolers on tables or in shelters while sleeping or while away hiking. Remove food from tables immediately after

Black begging at roadside park

A spoiled picnic

eating and store it in the car if at all possible. And do not cook in the tent: such odors are very attractive to bears. The ultimate in camp hygiene, however, may not deter a previously conditioned bear from searching for food in tents. The safest retreat in such a case is one's automobile.

Grizzly sow and cubs

The hiker in wilderness parts of the Rockies also should observe a few precautions. If only interested in hiking and scenery, try to avoid areas of known grizzly abundance. This information can usually be obtained from park rangers or others with local knowledge. Second, leave dogs at home. Bears often show a distinct dislike for dogs, particularly barking ones. A dog may be able to outrun a bear, but loyalty may bring it directly to its master, to whom the bear's attack is likely to be redirected. If one must take a dog along, keep it on a leash at all times. Third, make lots of noise, especially when droppings or tracks along the trail indicate you are in grizzly country, when vision is obstructed by trees or brush, and when noisy winds or rushing streams may prevent bears from easily hearing or smelling you. In this way you are not likely to surprise a sow with cubs at close range — the cause of most attacks. Loud talking, shouting, singing or various noise-makers such as stones in tin cans are effective. Even the belligerent female with cubs will normally move slowly away if warned of approaching humans. And last, when in areas where grizzlies are known to occur, make careful note of available trees which you can climb.

Grizzly bear—the reward of wilderness

Should you find yourself in the unenviable position of being confronted at close range by a threatening grizzly, headlong pursuit is not the answer unless you can reach a nearby tree (adult grizzlies cannot climb trees; black bears can). Grizzlies can outrun the best sprinter. Rapid movements should be avoided. Soft talking has sometimes seemed to calm alarmed bears. Usually such grizzlies are curious and will move away after having identified the intruder by scent or sight.

In known cases of attack, injury has usually been less when the person rolled in a ball on the ground and remained motionless. Struggling may result in increased aggression by the bear.

The grizzly has evolved for thousands of years as king of his domain. Although he has developed a healthy respect for hunters, fear of other beasts — including man — is not a normal part of his behavioral repertoire. He is a noble beast, worthy of our respect and protection. In a few wilderness areas, at least, man must play second fiddle.

Fang and Claw: Dogs and Cats

THEIR ECOLOGICAL PLACE

In contrast to hooved mammals, which are herbivores, and bears, which are omnivores, members of the cat and dog families, *Felidae* and *Canidae* are carnivores, meat eaters, preferring usually to capture live prey. These animals are ecologically known as "secondary consumers," since they prey on primary consumers which in turn eat the vegetation. These relationships result in the concept of the "food chain." Typical food chains in the Rockies include the vegetation-mule deer-mountain lion or wolf and the vegetation-snowshoe hare-lynx or golden eagle chains. Thus, carnivores sit at the top of the food chain. Because of that position, their numbers are relatively few compared to lower levels in the food chain. These species show many adaptations to the predatory way of life; for example, in mammals the teeth and jaw muscles are particularly well developed. Like their major prey species, they also are active all year.

Lynx with prey

MOUNTAIN CATS

Three wild members of the cat family may be encountered in the Rockies: the mountain lion, the lynx and the bobcat. Unfortunately they are secretive and seldom so co-operative as to allow their presence to be detected.

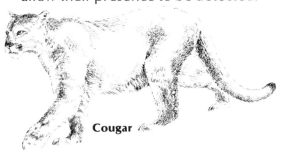

Cougar

Lynx

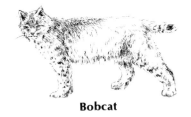

Bobcat

The mountain lion is not likely to be mistaken for any other animal because of its six to nine foot length of which about one-third is tail. The facial features are not unlike those of its domestic cousin. This mysterious and much persecuted feline has (or had) the distinction of having the most extensive distribution in the Western Hemisphere: from the Yukon-British Columbia border to Patagonia, and from Vancouver Island to New Brunswick and Florida. Remnant populations still exist in the latter two areas, but much of the former North American range is now vacant due to predator control, land settlement,

Cougar, King of the Mountains

...waits in silence

and loss of prey. Good numbers still exist in the western mountains, however, where four or five thousand, perhaps more, are thought to exist in each of the United States and Canada. Here their numbers are relatively stable, and they are gradually receiving much deserved better protection. Probably as a result of its wide distribution, the mountain lion also has been conferred many names: cougar, puma, panther, pointer, catamount, leon, or just lion.

Within the Rocky Mountain region the cougar is universally distributed, but is most abundant in the dry, semi-open Montane forests of the most inaccessible and rugged terrain. Even here they are so secretive that usually only their tracks or kills reveal their presence — just cause for being described as "the ghosts of North America." Probably only the wolf has had such a controversial history. The naturalist Ernest Thompson Seton referred to the lion as "lithe and splendid beasthood," but western ranchers were more severe. Even the avid conservationist Theodore Roosevelt saw fit to describe at least one mountain lion as a ". . . big horse-killing cat, the destroyer of the deer, the lord of stealthy murder . . ." With lion populations much reduced in stock raising areas today, such attitudes have largely been replaced by tolerance, and even by active preservation.

The two other cats occurring in the Rockies are the lynx and bobcat, readily distinguished from the mountain lion by their smaller size and very short tail, but quite similar to one another. The lynx, however, has large black ear tufts, large heavily furred feet, and longer legs than the bobcat. The tail of the lynx has a black tip which extends all the way around, while that of the bobcat is black only on the upper surface. Generally, though, different distribution ranges and habitat selection separate the two.

Lynx is at home in trees as on ground

Bobcat: note black tip does not circle tail

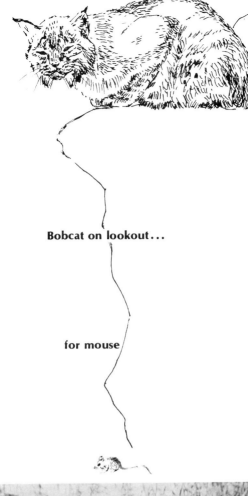

From their geographic distribution, we could almost call the lynx a Canadian cat and the bobcat an American, though some overlap happens, particularly in the Rocky Mountain region. There the bobcat extends into southern Canada, mostly in the foothills and adjacent plains, while the lynx extends southward to northern Colorado at higher elevations in the Subalpine Forest. Thus, where the two ranges overlap geographically, they are largely separated altitudinally and ecologically.

In our western mountains the bobcat is most likely observable in canyons and valleys where pinon, mountain mahogany, sagebrush and juniper grow. Here it hunts by day or night, and depends upon random searching and a keen sense of sight to obtain prey, principally rodents. The bobcat patiently stalks its quarry, taking advantage of available cover. At the proper time, a few swift leaps carry it onto the back of its unsuspecting victim. Bobcats also spend considerable time on high lookouts, waiting for prey to pass below. The bulk of its diet is small mammals: mice, rats, chipmunks, grand squirrels, rabbits, and so-on, but carrion birds, eggs and even insects may be consumed.

Bobcat on lookout...

for mouse

The lynx is not such a versatile feeder as its close relative the bobcat. In its spruce forest habitat, its population abundance is closely tied to that of its main food, the snowshoe hare. Cycles in hare abundance occur every nine to ten years, and the lynx thus follows suit — usually with a time lag of two to three years. In years immediately following hare population crashes, the lynx may be completely unsuccessful in raising any young, due to lack of sufficient food supply.

Lynx feeding on carrion

Large furred snowshoe-like feet of the lynx enable it to travel with ease over deep snow

The large furred snowshoe feet of the lynx enable it to travel with ease over deep snow. In winter its daily movements are three to six miles. Through following lynx tracks in winter, we have learned that about 15% of their attempts to capture hares are successful, and that their average rate of kill is about one animal every two or three nights.

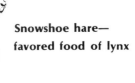

Snowshoe hare—
favored food of lynx

81

Deer constitute the main food source for most cougars. Rare indeed is the photo photographer Tom W. Hall has presented here!

MOUNTAIN LIONS

While seldom observed, the stealthy mountain lion, or cougar, is certainly the most important large carnivore in our western mountains, so it deserves special attention. This superbly adapted cat can drag down elk nearly ten times its own weight, and regularly takes mule deer two to three times its weight. Furthermore, cooperative hunting in packs, such as practised by wolves, is not a cougar trait. Unlike wolves, who rely on numbers and on speed to overtake their prey, the mountain lion moves stealthily very close to its intended prey before launching its final attack. With few exceptions, any animal placing itself in a vulnerable position is subject to cougar predation.

Recently, intensive scientific studies of mountain lions in the Idaho Primitive Area have added greatly to our understanding of this cat and its ecological relationships. In that rugged area the mountain lion is as abundant as anywhere in the Rockies, and populations of about one adult per twenty square miles can be expected. Including kittens, there is about one cougar for every six square miles of habitat. Regardless of the abundance of food, cougar numbers usually do not exceed this. Adults are firmly established on territories which are mutually respected, at least by members of the same sex. In winter, females have a home range of five to 25 square miles, while that of males is 15 to 30 square miles.

Cougars have no trouble recognizing the home ground of other adults because the resident cat will scrape together leaves, twigs or pine needles into mounds a few inches high and urinate on them. These "scrapes" are signposts which delineate the territory. They are usually under trees, on ridges, and at points where regularly used trails cross one another. Scientists who have tracked newcomers to scrapes of residents noted that the interlopers abruptly changed course, knowing that another cougar or family was in the vicinity, and retraced their steps for several miles before trying another area.

Cougars utilize scent in locating prey and identifying territories. Scraps of leaves are urinated on for signposts

This behavior has been termed "mutual avoidance," and has survival advantages for this solitary species. Being lone predators, mountain lions depend on individual strength and agility to survive. Fighting in defense of their territory, as do some social species like wolves, is a luxury cougars cannot afford. An injured wolf may survive because it is a member of a pack, while an injured solitary mountain lion would probably starve.

Female cougar and kitten

Since mountain lions are solitary creatures, the only lengthy social relationship is between mother and kittens. This lasts about two years, after which the juveniles must fend for themselves and disperse in search of an unoccupied territory. Social tolerance of adult males and females is exhibited only during the breeding season, a period of a few weeks usually in winter or early spring. However, these big felines, like their small domestic relatives, are capable of breeding at any time of the year. The cougar male is not a family animal. He neither sees nor takes part in the raising of his offspring. Females normally mate only with one male during each breeding period, but may mate with several different males during their lifetime.

Cougars mating

After a gestation period of about three months, the spotted kittens, usually two or three, are born in a cave or other natural den such as an uprooted tree. The newborn young are helpless and born with their eyes closed. The mother brings food to them in addition to providing milk, from which they are weaned at about two months, when kittens leave their natal den to enter the

Newborn cougar kitten still have eyes closed until about a week of age. Young are usually born under log or rock overhang

Five month old kitten spitting dislike

83

Day bed in hollow log

Cougar on coyote kill. While deer are the staple diet, a wide variety of animals is hunted including bighorn sheep, elk, goat, rabbits and beaver

Six month old cougar

world also. After this the family may use various temporary dens and caves, but they never again depend upon a home den.

Throughout its North American range the cougar is largely a predator of deer, whether black-tails on Vancouver Island, white-tails in New Brunswick, or mule deer in Idaho. However, other species are also taken. Studies in British Columbia show that moose and snowshoe hares can be important food in some areas, and that porcupines, beavers and grouse also are eaten. In Utah and Nevada, mule deer have been known to comprise 80% of the mountain lion diet, with porcupines, livestock, rabbits, beaver, squirrels, mice, wapiti, coyote, bobcat, skunk and grass making up the remainder.

In the Idaho Primitive Area, analysis of lion droppings has shown that mule deer and wapiti make up 70% of the prey, snowshoe hares about 5%, and with various small mammals and grass making up the remainder. Occasional kills of coyotes, bighorn sheep, and mountain goats were documented. These excellent studies show that mountain lions, despite their great strength and agility, kill mostly the young or aged deer and wapiti — the easiest prey. Among the older wapiti and mule deer, males were more vulnerable than females. Mountain lions actually cull the poorest specimens from the herds — the infirm and the aged — which leaves the strongest and best examples to survive and pass their characteristics to future generations. Further, many deer and wapiti taken by mountain lions in winter are likely suffering from malnutrition, and probably would die eventually of starvation if not taken by predators.

Mountain lion predation in the Idaho Primitive Area has another beneficial effect: keeping deer and wapiti herds on the move. This is desirable when food is scarce on the limited winter ranges. Researchers have discovered that the reaction of prey herds to a cougar kill is very striking. The deer and wapiti immediately abandon the kill area and move to new feeding grounds, increasing their chances of finding and using all available food resources.

Mountain lions may go without killing a big game animal for six to eight days or more. In the Idaho Primitive Area, adult cats kill a

The stalk

Cougar burying kill

deer every ten to fourteen days in winter, but this interval is probably longer when wapiti are taken. When a kill is made, mountain lions can and do eat a large quantity of meat in a short time. Like most wild cats, they are well adapted to a "feast or famine" regime. Cougar kills are covered with snow, sticks, or whatever is available to protect them from scavengers, and the lone cougar or family will normally return to them for several days until they are almost entirely consumed. In the Idaho studies it has been calculated that each adult mountain lion kills about 2,000 to 2,500 pounds of deer and wapiti per year, and that from five to seven wapiti or from 14 to 20 deer are required to sustain one adult for one year. Females with growing kittens are known to kill more. Even when subjected to this level of predation, however, deer and wapiti populations in the Primitive Area were shown to be on the increase, and are limited ultimately by the availability browse supply rather than by predation.

Predation, as illustrated by mountain lions and their prey in the Rockies, is a dynamic and integral aspect of the delicate balance of nature. The cougar itself is certainly a splendid part of any wilderness, a true vestige of primitive North America.

Cougar

WILD MOUNTAIN DOGS

Readers should not imply from the above title that our wild *canids,* foxes, coyotes and wolves — originated from domestic dogs, but only that they belong to the same family. Actually, domestic dogs originated from their wild relatives, primarily in Europe and Asia. Three species of the dog family occur in varied abundance in the Rockies: the timber wolf, the coyote, and the red fox. The grey fox, a more southern species, occurs in mountain valleys in the arid southwest but is not typical of the Rockies.

Red Fox

DOG FAMILY

Wolf

Coyote

85

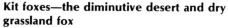

Kit foxes—the diminutive desert and dry grassland fox

The diminutive kit fox, an inhabitant of the western Great Plains from Alberta to Texas and the arid southwest, also may be found sporadically around the fringes of the Rockies, but will not be considered here.

Probably no mammal the world over has been as maligned and misrepresented as the wolf. The mythology of werewolves, fairy tales like Little Red Riding Hood, and fictional mis-representation of the animals as bloodthirsty killers of man and beast have served to develop a deep-seated fear of wolves from childhood onward in many human cultures. Although several well documented attacks on man by bears and a few by cougars are established facts, not a single authenticated attack on man by the so-called "fiendish" wolf has been recorded.

The wolf, however, is as intolerant of human civilization as we are of it. Like the cougar and grizzly, its range has greatly shrunk in North America from land settlement, clearing, agriculture and predator control spreading westward and northward across the continent. In the Rocky Mountain Region, one seldom encounters wolves south of Jasper National Park, although strays from Canada are sometimes reported in northern Idaho and Montana, and a remnant population may exist in Yellowstone National Park.

The wolf—a wilderness species intolerant of man

The dedicated wolf watcher is advised to try the Athabasca Valley or Sunwapta River areas in Jasper National Park in winter, or perhaps Mount Robson or Wells Gray Provincial Parks of British Columbia.

Wolf colors are quite varied, ranging from creamy white through gray to nearly black. Wolf packs in the Jasper Park area are commonly four to eight in size, although larger ones have been reported, and the packs' home ranges are from 50 to 100 square miles each. Individual movements of over 150 miles have been reported, and 15 to 20 mile daily hunting movements are quite common. Prey animals in the northern Rockies are primarily the big game species, of which wapiti and mule deer are most important. The wolf has shown great adaptability in its food

Wolf in pursuit of elk

Wolf pack on
moose kill

habits, specializing on the most available species from area to area, whether Arctic hare on Ellesmere Island, caribou on the Arctic mainland, bison in Wood Buffalo National Park, moose on Isle Royale, or white-tailed deer in Minnesota. Like the mountain lion, the wolf can gorge itself in a short time and then fast for several days. Wolves weighing little over 100 pounds have consumed 35 pounds of meat in one day.

In contrast with the cougar, wolf life is social and co-operative. In the Rockies, mating occurs in March and the pups are born

Premating displays of wolves

about two months later. Birth and early life take place in deep dens dug into the ground by each mother who then seldom leaves the den during the first few weeks after giving birth. Food is brought to the den site, or cached near it, by any members of the pack which consist of one or more family groups. The pack does much of its hunting at night and may lounge near the den during the day. Pack members are very attentive to the pups once outside the den, and tolerate their playful exuberance to a degree not often seen in humans. The pack, including new offspring, leave the maternal den site about midsummer and frequently congregate and socialize during late summer at places dubbed "rendezvous sites" by biologists. Here there is much

Curious wolf pup

Wolves are social animals and even sleeping
is done in groups

socializing, utilizing several well-developed means of wolf communication: facial expressions, tailwagging, and howling. This probably serves to establish or reaffirm a well-developed dominance order and social structure in the pack.

The most direct contact humans may expect to have with wolves is to hear the spine-tingling howls. For most, this will be sufficient to affirm that a true wilderness, and a true representative of it, still exists on our ravaged continent.

The howl—

Red foxes

Red fox digging a den

The red fox and coyote are found throughout the area, but are abundant nowhere. Typical of the dog family, red foxes mate in winter, the female digs a den in a secluded area, and after a gestation period of 52 days four to nine pups are born in a period between mid-March and mid-April. Blind for their first ten days, the cubs remain in the den for a month. They are weaned at three months, but until then they are guarded and fed by their parents. Social behavior is less developed than in the wolves':

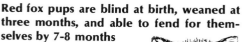
Red fox pups are blind at birth, weaned at three months, and able to fend for themselves by 7-8 months

88

Young red foxes

at four months, when the young red foxes are almost full grown, they leave the den area, fending for themselves after their first autumn.

A creature of the open meadowlands, the red fox hunts and eats a wide variety of foods. Although the animal is omnivorous, 90 per cent of its diet is composed normally of mice and other small rodents, but all kinds of vegetation, juicy green shoots, berries, grasshoppers and other insects round out its larder.

Where prey species are cyclic and numbers fluctuate from year to year, fox population density also fluctuates. When staple foods

Fox pursues varying hare—staple diet is mice and other small mammals but some berries and grasses are eaten. When staples are scarce he often invades farmyards

like mice and other rodents are in low numbers, foxes often invade farmyards, carrying off chickens, thus earning for themselves an evil reputation as thieves. Despite this, the swift and cunning red foxes manage to elude poisons, guns and traps, and their numbers have not diminished.

Fox digging in snow

Like bears, the "red" fox can show a confusing array of coat colors, even within one litter. The basic color is red, but "cross", "black" and "silver" color phases can occur. The "cross" fox is browner or darker than the red, and the "black" is black all over, two extreme variations possible from the red phase. The "silver" phase has a black coat with white-tipped fur and, although it occurs in the wild, was bred selectively by fur farmers during the heyday of women's apparel made from fox fur.

Red foxes come in many color phases—red, black, silver and cross

THE CLEVER COYOTE

One of the loneliest sounds in the world is the howl of a coyote perched on the moonlit rim of a mountain canyon. Coyotes are sometimes confused with true wolves because of their similar dog-like appearance. However, the coyote is less than half the size of the wolf, and has a bushy tail which usually droops when it lopes along instead of being held in the more erect position of the wolf. Despite its common title "prairie wolf," the coyote (whose name comes from the Aztec word *coyotl)* also ranges high into the mountains, occasionally being found above timberline in the dead of winter.

The clever coyote has proved to be one of North America's more adaptable mammals. Instead of retreating before the forces of human occupation, it merely changed its lifestyle and remained in areas where civilization drove out many less adaptable animals. Where the great wolf and grizzly failed, the coyote has succeeded. This trait was apparently recognized long ago, principally in the popular Indian legend in which storytellers prophesied that the coyote will be the last animal on earth.

A pair of coyotes

Coyote pups

More socially developed than red foxes, coyotes like wolves mate for life. Coyotes breed in February, and after a gestation period of about 63 days the five or six young are born in a secluded underground den. Like red fox kits, coyote pups are born blind and their eyes open by their tenth day; however, in other ways their development is more rapid and they leave the family den in five to six weeks. By July or August the young coyotes are old enough to learn the arts of hunting and self-preservation while running with their parents.

Within the Rocky Mountain region the coyote has had to change his ways less than on the adjacent plains. Here its tolerance for *Homo sapiens* is evident again, however, through his casual attention to human observers. Particularly in the larger parks and refuges, the coyote may be observed at close range going about his daily business of pouncing on mice or frogs, or of patrolling the campground just after dark to pick up scraps which have fallen from picnic tables. In civilized areas where they are

Coyote on the hunt for rodents

In many parks the adaptable coyotes have learned to beg food from visitors

hunted, coyotes are very wary and may flee rapidly upon hearing the distant sounds of jeeps, snowmobiles or aircraft, depending upon which is the usual transport of local hunters. Some have learned by experience to recognize a gun by sight. Although chiefly nocturnal (active at night) in settled areas, the coyote is seen by day commonly in the National Parks.

Poisoned, trapped and hunted for decades, numbers of the coyote are little diminished today. In earlier years they were controlled even in the National Parks. Studies in Yellowstone Park suggest that during the long period when two or three hundred were destroyed annually in the park, numbers remained high. When artificial control was stopped in 1935, many people expected a great increase in their numbers. According to biologists, however, they continued to be common, but were no more plentiful than when poisoning was carried out.

Feeding habits of the coyote have been studied in several areas, including Jasper and Yellowstone National Parks. Results show they feed on a much wider variety of prey than the more specialized larger carnivores (wolf, cougar) but that they have their staples also. Meadow mice or "voles" are the most consistent food source in both parks, but hares, ground squirrels, pocket gophers, porcupines, beavers, marmots and a few small birds are regularly taken depending upon local availability. A good deal of carrion, mostly consisting of the remains of big game animals killed by larger predators is also consumed, as are some animals which have died of starvation. Forest dwelling mice, chipmunks and squirrels seldom occur in coyote fare, indicating its preference for hunting in meadows and other open areas. Frogs, insects, berries and fruits round out diet.

Poisoned coyotes—the victims of 1080

Search pattern of coyote looking for mice beneath snow

Coyotes feeding on road kill

The jaws of the coyote reflect his versatility as predator and scavenger. Some of his molars are sharp for tearing meat—others flat for grinding bones

Occasionally, coyotes have been known to kill live game animals such as deer but only when such prey is on its last legs from malnutrition. One instance of a coyote being killed by an elk was reported in Yellowstone. Wolves and cougars are known to be intolerant of coyotes and occasionally kill them, but diseases such as mange and rabies seem the most important controls of coyote numbers. These diseases may reach epidemic proportions when coyote populations are at a high level and malnutrition is prevalent.

91

Marten

Striped skunk skull

Precious Fur: The Weasel Family

While not commonly observed, certain members of the weasel family (*Mustelidae*) are important members of the Rocky Mountain fauna. Among them are weasels, mink, marten, fisher, wolverine, badger, otter and skunk. Like the cat and dog families already discussed, these mammals are carnivores, largely subsisting by predation on other animals. However, food habits vary considerably, and some species, such as skunks, are almost omnivorous.

Like other meat eaters, members of this family have teeth well developed for tearing and shearing flesh. All species have five toes on each foot, each with a nonretractile claw. All have tails, but these vary in length. Well developed musk glands in the anal region are a prominent family characteristic. All mustelids have such glands, but they are best known in skunks, the only species to use them as defensive weapons. Size of the family members varies greatly, from the diminutive least weasel weighing less than two ounces, to the wolverine which may reach 40 pounds, a disparity of over 300 times. The ferocious least weasel, weighing little more than a large meadow vole, is the smallest beast of prey on the continent. Another intriguing feature of the family is its long gestation period — up to one year — the result of a phenomenon known as delayed implantation (See *Reproductive Oddities*).

Mustelids are not very social animals, the only common group being a family, and this is short-lived. Hunting is a singular pursuit, and most activity is at night. The sense of smell is highly developed and most important for their predatory activity. Pound for pound, the mustelid family members, particularly the weasels and their close cousin the mink, are among the most capable and efficient killers in the animal world. Since they are relatively small and highly energetic creatures, their food demands are so great that almost all their active time is spent in pursuit of prey.

Weasel wrapped around egg so it can puncture shell and suck out contents

Except for the badger and skunk in the colder parts of their range, mustelids are active all year: they do not hibernate. The change to a white winter coat is exhibited only by the weasels in the snowier parts of their range, which includes the Rocky Mountain region.

Most of the mustelids are widespread in North America, thus none are considered truly a Rocky Mountain species. Due to the onslaught of civilization, however, the Rockies have become an important refuge. The eleven species occurring in and around this region vary greatly in abundance, and the closely related species have generally sorted themselves into different habitats to avoid competition.

The diminutive least weasel, little known and very rare throughout its range, has not been reported in the Rockies south of Glacier National Park. At the southern extreme, the spotted skunk inhabits the region's fringes in southern Idaho, extreme southwest Montana, southern Wyoming and Colorado. It prefers brushy areas away from dense forest, and will most often be encountered in the lower, more arid valleys, seldom above 6,500 feet.

The least weasel—the smallest predator of warm blooded prey on the continent

Spotted skunk

Two species, the long-tailed weasel and badger, are primarily animals of the plains, farmlands, dry valleys and forest openings, but are widespread in the region, sometimes occurring above timberline. Badgers have been seen to prey on yellow-bellied marmots at 10,500 feet on Beartooth Plateau in Wyoming. Powerful diggers, they should be looked for in open and semi-open valleys and foothills where they prey extensively on burrowing rodents such as ground squirrels and pocket gophers. However, being nocturnal, they are not commonly seen by day. Good habitats exist in the broad valleys of Yellowstone and Grand Teton National Parks, and in more restricted areas north as far as Banff.

The badger—a powerful digger

The long-tailed or prairie weasel has similar distribution and habitat to the badger, occurring north to about Jasper. It is a creature of grassland, parkland, and semi-open forest where it preys largely on mice, but rabbits, pikas, pocket gophers, ground squirrels and small birds are also taken.

Long-tailed or prairie weasel

Forest dwelling mustelids are probably most typical of the Rockies even if widespread across the Boreal forest. These include the short-tailed weasel, marten, fisher, wolverine, and mink.

Short-tailed weasel or ermine in white winter coat with prey

The short-tailed weasel, known as ermine when in its white winter coat, occurs throughout this region primarily in the coniferous forest zone. Within this zone it often frequents rockslides, streambanks and shrubby meadows. Here it is mostly a "mouser", but a variety of small prey may be taken including birds, frogs, grasshoppers and even worms. Weasel abundance varies greatly from place to place and year to year according to the ups and downs of their major prey. Population levels of about ten per square mile have been reported at Jasper Park.

Weasels are speedy agile creatures with a great deal of curiosity. They are often described as bloodthirsty, and are even reported to live by sucking the blood of their prey. These claims are exaggerated. However, the perpetually hungry weasel often does kill much more than it can eat, particularly when confronted with a bonanza.

Weasels have devised a highly successful manner of procuring and killing their catch. A rapid dash, the luckless prey is bitten at the back of the skull, the forelegs encircle the prey as if hugging it, while the hind legs are brought up to scratch wildly at the captive. Thus the predator largely avoids retaliation and can change its grip without losing the prey should the initial attack not be immediately fatal.

Short-tailed weasel in brown summer pelage

Diminutive weasel wraps its body around rabbit while it maintains death grip on prey's throat

The inquisitive weasel

Pine marten eating mouse

The marten, better known to fur fanciers as sable, is a true forest dweller largely confined to the Subalpine and upper Montane forest zones in the Rockies. Being larger than the weasel (about three or four pounds) it can take larger prey. But still its staple fare is mice. Its adeptness in trees and frequent association with squirrel nests have results in a reputation for feeding on tree squirrels. Marten food habits, however, do not bear this out. Studies in Banff, Glacier (Montana), and Grand Teton National parks have all shown mice to be the most important foods, particularly meadow and red-backed voles. In Glacier Park, red squirrel remains showed up in only four per cent of over 1,700 marten droppings. The eminent naturalist Adolph Murie found that marten in the mountains at Grand Teton fed largely on voles, pikas and jumping mice, although blueberries were also much relished. Many droppings contained nothing but blueberries. In pine forest near the open sagebrush country, ground

Pine Marten

squirrels and voles were eaten, whereas voles, pocket gophers, hawthorn and rhamnus berries predominated in the woods along the Snake River. So much for the tree squirrel myth.

The marten extends southward in the Subalpine forests of the main range of the Rockies to about the Colorado-New Mexico border Curious and very easily trapped, its population was much reduced in earlier years but is coming back well under present day protection. In good habitat, populations may reach five or more per square mile. They are not migratory and have small home ranges. During studies in Glacier Park, Montana, researchers captured one male 77 times on the same six-square-mile study area. Marten are frequently active during the day, but not easily observed despite this.

The fisher or pekan is also a forest dweller at home on ground or high in trees

Fisher

The marten's larger cousin, the fisher or pekan, is also a forest dweller, but is very rare by comparison. Range of the fisher in the Rockies extends south only to southern Montana, and this is a result of reintroductions. While probably never abundant, fishers were almost completely trapped out in the Rockies before 1900. Being creatures of habit, they have been slow to leave established home ranges in the north to repopulate former habitats. They are listed as exceedingly rare in Jasper Park, and their occurrence at Banff has not been firmly established.

In Montana the fisher was extinct before 1911. Thirty-six fishers were live-trapped in central British Columbia then released at three Montana sites in 1959 and 1960. Even under protection a number of these animals and their offspring were accidentally taken in traps set for mink, wolverine, bobcat and lynx, attesting to their extreme vulnerability to trapping. Trapped fishers were taken up to six years after release, and up to 64 miles from the release sites. Despite this, the introduction seems to have been successful — a tribute to conservation officials. Fishers are extinct in Yellowstone, Grand Teton, and Rocky Mountain National Parks.

Larger than its close relative the marten, the fisher can and does take larger prey, although mice are still important. Porcupines are a favorite food, and squirrels, chipmunks, hares and grouse are sometimes taken. Like the marten, the fisher is an adept tree climber, and largely restricts itself to the densely forested mountain slopes and valleys where it finds its prey.

Fisher

Wolverine

A still larger, more aggressive forest dwelling mustelid is the notorious wolverine, known by many names including glutton, carcajou, skunk-bear, and Indian devil. Its evil reputation results from its habits of robbing traplines, devouring food larders in trappers' cabins, and fouling cabin contents with its musk. In addition, the wolverine is quite difficult to trap.

The wolverine is a tough customer leading a tough life. Ranging in the most rugged and inhospitable parts of the upper Sub-alpine forest and adjacent Alpine Tundra, it must contend with extreme cold, deep snow, and scarcity of prey. Thus, wolverine numbers are fairly low throughout their range, which includes the Rockies south to about Yellowstone National Park. In the Canadian Rockies, they are relatively abundant. In Montana, wolverines were near extinction by 1920, but have been increasing under better protection since about 1940. Since then they have recolonized most of their former range in Montana without the aid of reintroductions by man. The original colonizers evidently moved into Glacier Park from Canada, then moved southward from there. A few probably also occur in Idaho, adjacent to the Montana border.

Wolverines, which average only 25 to 30 pounds in weight, occasionally kill big game animals, ordinarily only when the predator has an advantage. Game animals on which they prey are usually starving or trapped by deep snow. Carrion also forms a large part of the animal's diet, and while much of the carrion is carcasses of game animals which have died of disease, malnutrition and accidents, the wolverine will also take prey killed by larger predators. Snowshoe hares are also important food in winter. In summer, the wolverine eats mice, ground squirrels, marmots, porcupines, beavers, birds and blueberries.

In order to hide and preserve prey the wolverine often drags prey great distances to bury it in a snow bank or store it up a tree

The hardy, pugnacious wolverine, despite the vicissitudes of its Arctic-Alpine environment, gives birth to its young in late February and March when temperatures may be below zero and snow depths at their greatest. Young are born and nursed in dens which are dug in the snow above ground surface. Snowfilled ravines above timberline often serve this purpose.

Two other members of the weasel family, the mink and otter, are usually found in or near the water. The sleek and playful river otter occurs from coast to coast and throughout the region, but is not abundant in the Rockies. He is found only along the major rivers and lakes where his aquatic foods — fish, frogs, crayfish and mussels are plentiful. The otter is more abundant west of the continental divide than to the east, notably along the major valleys. Fairly good habitats include Bowron Lakes, Wells Gray Park, and the Creston area in British Columbia, Thompson Lakes and Red Rock Lakes in Montana, and the many lakes in Yellowstone and Grand Teton National Parks.

Crustaceans and fish are the main fare of the agile otter

The river otter fishes, travels and plays in the water, but resides on land, usually in dens under the roots of large trees or near the water among large boulders. Where a family of otters is in residence, their sign will be plentiful and obvious. They forage along the shores, leaving ample evidence of their presence in the form of well-defined trails, plus droppings containing the remains of fish and crustaceans.

The ubiquitous mink occupies similar habitat to the otter, but spends less time in the water and more on the shore. Mink are more abundant and widespread in the Rockies than the otter, and can be encountered almost anywhere, but normally occupy the middle and lower elevations, chiefly along the shores of streams, lakes and marshes. Mink, being more adaptable, do not confine their diet to fish, and other important foods are frogs, snakes, insects, birds, eggs, muskrats and mice.

Mink also are water frequenting mammals but spend much time on land in search of frogs, insects, eggs and nesting birds

Striped skunk— an omnivore eating various succulent plants, worms, eggs, and carrion

The striped skunk is widespread in the Rockies and often encountered around townsites, cabins and campgrounds where it can scavenge for food. Usual habitats in the Rockies include lower elevation forests, aspen groves, brushy bottomlands and mixed forest along rivers and streams. Skunks are highly omnivorous and not efficient predators. Their list of foods is long and changes greatly with the seasons. Insects are very important as well as fruits and other vegetable matter. Worms, birds' eggs, frogs, a few small mammals and birds, carrion and garbage make up much of the remainder.

The striped skunk family maintains contact through scent trails

MUSK GLANDS — PERFUME AND PROTECTION

Most mammals have scent glands of one kind or another, and these are particularly well developed in the weasel family. In predatory and forest dwelling non-social mammals occurring in small numbers, which are seldom in visual contact, scent is particularly important to advertise the home range or territory of individuals. In addition, it may serve to maintain contact of mother and offspring, or to bring prospective mates together at the appropriate time of year. No doubt scent glands serve this function in the mustelids as well. One well known species (too well known to the unfortunate few), the skunk, has evolved one step further and can utilize his anal scent glands for defense. Curiously, skunks and several other species, such as civets and mongooses, which use scent glands for defense are brightly striped rather than protectively colored. It seems these animals not only lack need for camouflage, but prefer to advertise their presence. In this way the prospective enemy or competitor usually retreats, so the previous musk is fired only as a last resort. The striped skunk's anal glands are large, and their fetid contents can be shot out with astonishing accuracy to a distance of about twelve feet. Skunks normally assume threatening attitudes before letting fly with their malodorous missile; striped skunks stamp their feet, arch their back, raise their tail, and orient their dangerous rear end toward the intruder. This is usually sufficient

A great defense without bark or bite

to deter any creature familiar with skunks, but many dogs, unfamiliar with the codes of the wild, insist on learning the hard way. Some never learn at all. Humans may find that stepping on a skunk in thick bush while searching for duck nests is sufficient harassment to warrant a discharge of the acrid, yellowish musk which can not only penetrate two pairs of pants to the skin, but is revived upon taking each bath for several days thereafter. Rubbing on tomato juice is the best treatment to remove the odor from one's skin. Impregnated clothing is best hung out-of-doors for several weeks, or destroyed.

Spotted skunk—when threatened stands on its forefeet

MANY ADAPTATIONS

The variety of niches occupied by members of the weasel family have required a certain amount of adaptation on the animals' part during the course of evolution.

Coping with winter in the Rockies involves growing a heavy, lustrous coat, the downfall of several mustelids of value to the fur trade. Rocky Mountain weasels turn white in winter, providing concealment from avian predators as well as allowing their own predatory activities to proceed largely undetected. White coloration also radiates less heat and is thus important for heat conservation. The sinuous body form of weasels is well adapted to following their prey into burrows or crevices, and even for pursuit under a deep covering of snow. Skunks and badgers in the Rockies normally hibernate to avoid the worst of winter when their main foods are mostly unavailable.

Long-tailed weasel—in early fall the white winter pelage starts to grow in

The myopic badger is well developed for an underground or *fossorial* existence. Its stout, muscular body, powerful legs and long claws are well adapted to digging for its supper. The badger's cousins, the marten and fisher, are equally well adapted for tree life. They have hand-like feet, the toes of which are long and flexible, supplemented by sharp, strong claws especially adapted for clutching the rough bark of a tree. As well as arboreal and fossorial leanings, the weasel family has aquatic tendencies. The streamlined, compact body of the otter with its stout muscular tail enables it to swim with speed and agility. Its legs are short, the hind feet are well webbed, and the fur is short and fine, allowing ease of movement through water. In addition, the eyes are located high on the head to allow good vision while swimming.

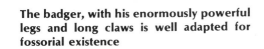
The badger, with his enormously powerful legs and long claws is well adapted for fossorial existence

REPRODUCTIVE ODDITIES

Several mammals display the phenomenon of *delayed implantation,* which seems most common in the weasel family. In such mammals the eggs are fertilized during the usual breeding season, but the fertilized eggs, *blastocysts,* do not attach to the wall of the uterus, or womb, for several months. A very long period of gestation results, almost a full year for some mustelids. Once the blastocysts do attach, or "implant" development of the embryos is very rapid, usually about one month.

Weasels in entwined mating position

Fishers, for example, mate in late March and early April, but the fertilized eggs do not implant and begin development for almost 11 months. The foetuses develop rapidly over about a 30-day period in February and March, and most births occur from late February to early April, with a peak in March. Mating occurs again immediately following birth of the litter. Most mammals cannot be bred successfully while they are nursing a litter, but this does not apply to many members of the weasel family.

Pine martens sleeping

The mustelids, particularly the larger species, are not highly prolific mammals. This is generally typical of predators which have few natural enemies and are fairly long-lived. The mink appears to be somewhat of an exception, however, and so deserves its reputation for fecundity. Mink are polygamous, have a short gestation period (about 50 days), large litters (three to ten) and may be sexually mature at five or six months of age. They are thus well adapted for the fur farm industry.

Mink mother teaches young to forage and hunt

100

Rabbits and Their Kin

Snowshoe skull

Pika skull

This group, known scientifically as *lagomorphs,* includes rabbits, hares, and pikas. The comical little pika, alias "cony" or "rock rabbit," is a widespread and typical resident of the Rockies, occurring southward to northern New Mexico. Outwardly, the pika shows little resemblance to the rabbit, but the relationship is clear when skulls and teeth are compared. However, more representative members of the group are cottontail rabbits, jackrabbits, and snowshoe hares.

In the west cottontails are animals of low, brushy valleys, not of the high mountains. Three species occur in and around the mountain regions, but all are to be found south of the Canadian border. The desert cottontail is a rabbit of low valleys and desert, again, mostly to the south, where it occurs throughout most parts of Colorado and in low dry valleys along the eastern flank of the Rockies north to the Missouri River in Montana. West of the Rockies, the pygmy cottontail rabbit occupies similar sagebrush habitat in Idaho, Nevada, and extreme south-western Montana. These two species are largely peripheral to the Rockies and cannot be considered typical. A third species, the mountain cottontail is somewhat more typical because it is distributed widely from southwestern Montana to southern Colorado, mainly in brushy valleys among dry forests of the lower Montane and Foothills zones.

Cottontail rabbit—a common North American species with several varieties found in bushy areas of the Rocky Mountains

The jackrabbits, which are really hares, differ from the cottontails, being larger in size, with longer ears and bigger feet. In contrast to the forest dwelling snowshoe hare and brush dwelling cottontails, the jackrabbits are creatures of the open, relatively flat grassland with scant cover. They rely primarily on high speed or underground burrows for protection. Jackrabbits are not characteristic Rocky Mountain mammals, but two species do occur in the region. The black-tailed jackrabbit is the common hare of the southwestern deserts, intermountain basins and dry valleys, occurring mainly in dry grassy valleys along the lower west slope of the Rockies from central Idaho to southeastern Colorado. It appears to have recently colonized extreme southwestern Montana. Its cousin, the white-tailed jackrabbit, has a more northerly distribution and so is more common in the region. It occurs in grassy valleys and foothills along both slopes of the Rockies from about Waterton Lakes National Park, Alberta, to southern Colorado. This large hare is brownish gray in summer but turns white or pale gray in winter. Its tail is all white. It has been clocked at speeds up to 34 miles per hour.

White-tailed jackrabbit frequents open plains

Snowshoe or varying hare

The snowshoe hare is the most typical Rocky Mountain lago-morph. This medium-sized species occurs from coast to coast in the northern Boreal forest, and extends southward in the Sub-alpine spruce-fir forest and associated stands of lodgepole pine and aspen to northern New Mexico. Its general distribution is quite similar to that of lynx, its major predator.

NATURE'S HAYMAKERS

One of the most delightful and characteristic mammals of the western mountains is the tiny pika. It is found throughout the region, but is extremely selective about its habitat. Pikas are not to be seen just anywhere. Rockslides, otherwise known as talus slopes, are the only home of pikas although they will travel short distances into nearby meadows or brush to procure food consisting entirely of vegetation. Many writers have characterized the pika as an Alpine mammal, but their elevational range of distribution is too great. They are known to occur as low as the 2,500 foot level along the Fisher River in Montana; in many areas they extend their range to well above timberline.

Pika—the rock rabbit of high talus slopes. The pika's gray brown coloration blends in well with surrounding lichen covered rocks

The pika is not likely to be confused with any other mammal. Aside from its specialized habitat, pika characteristics include small size (about six ounces in weight and six to eight inches long) no visible tail, and short round ears. While more closely related to rabbits than to rats, mice or squirrels, pikas do not have the rabbit's powerful hind legs. Fore and hind legs are about the same size. Its coloration is grayish to buffy brown and blends amazingly well with the boulders among which it finds protection. The only other mammals sometimes found in similar haunts, certain marmots and ground squirrels, are larger and have distinctive tails.

The pika has evolved an interesting strategy for survival in its harsh mountain environment. It neither hibernates like many high mountain rodents, nor scurries about searching for food all year like its distant cousins the hares. It prefers instead to gather a large cache of food during the short summer which it stores in its rocky hideaway for winter sustenance. Pikas are active only during the day, remaining so all year round, although winter activity is confined to the den and its immediate vicinity.

During the short mountain summers the pikas gather great quantities of fresh grasses and flowers. These are dried in the sun and then stored in underground ice chambers to keep fresh

Observers have noted that pikas gather and utilize a wide variety of plants. As summer draws to a close they are particularly busy scurrying from nearby meadows to their rockslides with mouths full of favorite forage. This vegetation is picked green and placed in little piles here and there on the rocks near the winter den so that it will cure in the sun. These odd looking little haystacks are sure evidence that bustling pikas are close at hand. With care, the haystack owner may also be observed at one of his favorite occupations: sunning himself on an exposed rock.

Pika taking a sun bath must be alert to predators

The hay piles are popularly considered to consist of grass, but in fact many plants are used. Careful studies show that leaves and stems from various herbs and shrubs make up about 80% of the food cache, while seeds and grasslike plants comprise about equal proportions of the remainder. Commonly used plants in southwestern Colorado include ferns, sedges, hellebore, lily of the valley, aspen, willow, mountain ash, serviceberry, meadow rue, columbine, clover, bluebells, avens and fleabanes. During feeding pikas tend to make short rapid forays from the talus slopes, rarely straying more than five meters.

Pika giving alarm call

In Colorado, the pika breeding season begins in late April and May, but may continue until July. Most females bear two litters per year. Mid-June is the average birth date of the first litter, with the second coming about a month later. Litters vary from one to six, with three being the most frequent size. The tiny young grow rapidly and are weaned when they are three to four weeks old. The second litter is conceived soon after the birth of the first, and born immediately following weaning of the earlier litter. Observers in Alberta have noted that young pikas are active out of the nests by their third week.

The pika is a noisy bundle of energy, and if you locate its food piles you will probably hear its alarm call. Its short but shrill squeaks have been likened to a rusty hinge and have a ventriloquistic effect which may be very confusing. Often the apparently distant squeak is actually coming from under one's feet, deep within the boulder pile.

A search for the hardy pika is a must for Rocky Mountain hikers, and such a search becomes even more rewarding in the spectacular landscapes occupied by this mountain mammal.

WINTER WHITECOATS

Casual mention has been made in previous sections about the protective nature of white pelage in winter, which serves most commonly as camouflage, protecting prey from predators. In some cases, however, nature also has provided predators, such as polar bears and snowy owls, with white winter disguises which allow them to approach prey undetected.

Snowshoe hare adapts to winter snow by growing a white coat...

and by having large feet for walking on snow

Within the region under discussion, the only mammals to stay white year-round are mountain goats. Others which turn white in winter are the weasels and hares. Among these, the aptly named snowshoe hare also possesses very large hind feet, the soles of which develop a pad of long, stiff, densely packed hairs in winter. This increases the surface area of each hind foot to as much as fourteen square inches, enabling this inhabitant of deep snow country to travel easily in winter. Man, it seems, was not the original inventor of snowshoes.

The duration of the hare's white winter coat is directly related to the period of snow cover on the ground. In the high arctic, hares are white all year. Snowshoe hares in the coastal areas of Washington state do not turn white at all. Within the Rocky Mountain region, the duration of winter whiteness varies with latitude and altitude. Hares at high elevations in the northern Rockies turn white earlier and stay white longer than others

Partially moulted varying hare

farther south or at lower elevations. The protective color changes in pelage seem not to be correlated with immediate weather changes, but rather with the average duration of snow. If winter comes late in any particular place, one may see patchy or even all white hares hopping conspicuously about on snowless ground. A late snow melt also may result in conspicuous brown hares on a snowy background in spring. Even on the same mountain, hares at higher elevations turn white significantly earlier than those lower down.

Hare in the high country

Varying hare in winter white pelage

Change in pelage color is accomplished by shedding one coat and growing a new one; the individual hairs do not change color. This molt occupies a period of several weeks in fall and spring. Consistent timing of the molt each year is believed synchronized through day length changing, or photoperiod.

CYCLES IN ABUNDANCE

The prolific snowshoe hare has been long renowned for the ups and downs of its abundance. Population levels for the same area have been determined to vary more than one hundredfold over a period of years. Biologists also have determined that the duration between two highs or two lows is fairly regular, about nine or ten years, thus the term *ten year cycle*. To be properly termed a *cycle*, peaks in abundance should recur at regular intervals as opposed to random fluctuations. Two major cycles of wildlife abundance are known for North America: the three-year cycle of lemmings on the tundra, and the ten-year cycle of snowshoe hares, ruffed grouse, and their predators in the Boreal and Subalpine forests.

Young varying hare

Young hares

**Lynx
—the main predator on hares**

Factors responsible for the ten-year cycle have been hotly debated for fifty years, and have included sun spots, psychological stress, weather, and epidemic diseases. It now appears, however, that food is the most important factor.

Explaining the snowshoe hare's population increase is not difficult: they breed at an early age, and commonly produce four litters per year about 36 days apart. Litters vary from two to seven, with an average of three to five. The young are born fully furred and with eyes open. They begin feeding on green food almost immediately. Studies in Alberta show that each adult female produced an average of eight to nineteen young per year, and that population density can reach 1,200 hares per square mile. At such levels, however, the food supply is soon exhausted,

resulting in population decline. During the decline phase adult survival is poor: their reproductive rate is about half normal, and less than 5% of young hares survive their first winter.

The lynx cycle crashes about one year after the hare crash

An interesting result of this hare cycle is its effect on the predators which rely on hares for sustenance — particularly the lynx. In fact, the ten-year cycle was first brought to light through the pronounced but regular changes in abundance of Canadian lynx pelts purchased by the Huson Bay Company. Accurate fur catch records kept since 1820 show regular nine to ten year peaks in the lynx catch, low years producing less than 4,000 pelts and high years yielding 25,000 to 60,000. These lynx population cycles correspond very well with those of their main prey — the hare. Such is the fate of a specialist which relies heavily on a single kind of food.

Busy Summer Folk: The Squirrel Family

Members of the squirrel family are among the most common and observable mammals of the Rocky Mountains. They are usually quite abundant within their normal ranges, mostly active during daylight hours, and seem quite tolerant of man's intrusions. In many parks and reserves they have become quite tame, frequenting campsites and even bumming for handouts, thus providing a fascinating opportunity for observation and study.

The group, known as the family *Sciuridae*, includes marmots, ground squirrels, tree squirrels, flying squirrels, chipmunks, and prairie dogs. Size varies from a length of about seven or eight inches and weight of two ounces in the case of the least chipmunk, to the hoary marmot's 25 or 30 inches and ten to 25 pounds. All species have short but distinct ears (often slightly tufted) well furred tails (sometimes very bushy) and four toes on the front feet, and five on the hind. All are vegetarians with fairly prominent incisors and no canine teeth.

Members of the family occupy a wide range of habitats from prairie, scrubland and dense forest to Alpine barrens. They have developed adaptations for fossorial (burrowing), arboreal (tree living), and volant (gliding) ways of life. The flying squirrel is strictly nocturnal, but all other species are active during the day.

Golden mantled ground squirrel begs a handout

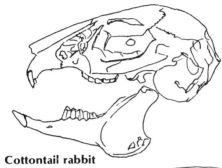

Cottontail rabbit

SKULLS

Golden mantled ground squirrel

Woodchuck

Hoary marmot

Two marmots, the hoary or whistler and the yellowbelly or rockchuck, are common in the western mountains, while a third, the common woodchuck of eastern North America, may occur locally in northwestern Alberta and eastern British Columbia. The large hoary marmot lives in small colonies in rockslides or boulder strewn meadows in the Alpine zone or among the upper reaches of the Subalpine spruce-fir forest. It is a hardy animal distributed from northern Alaska south into Montana and Idaho. The southern limit of the whistler's range is the Beaverhead Mountains in Montana. They are spotty in distribution, but Jasper, Banff, Yoho, and Glacier National Parks are good places

Yellow-bellied marmots

to begin a search. A southern counterpart of the whistler, the more yellowish and slightly smaller yellowbellied marmot occurs from the southern interior of British Columbia and extreme southwestern Alberta to northern New Mexico. In the northern part of its range it occupies dry valleys and open mountain slopes at lower and middle elevations, but farther south can be found in Alpine habitats together with pikas and Richardson's ground squirrel. Marmots have a short above-ground period, and are most likely to be seen sunning themselves on exposed rocks from May to July.

Columbian ground squirrel

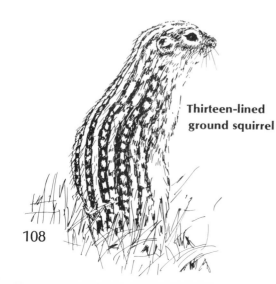

Uinta ground squirrel

The ground squirrels will be readily recognized because they are smaller than marmots, larger than chipmunks, and inhabit burrows in fairly open country. Only three kinds, the Columbian, Richardson's, and golden mantled ground squirrels are common and widespread in the Rockies, while a fourth, the Uinta ground squirrel, is more localized in southwestern Montana, western Wyoming, southwestern Idaho, and northeastern Utah. Several other closely related species occur around the fringe of the Rocky Mountain area. One of these, the widespread thirteen-lined ground squirrel of the Great Plains, may occasionally be encountered in grassy valleys along the eastern flank of the Rockies, while the large grey rock squirrel inhabits rocky arid valleys as far north as central Colorado on both sides of the Continental Divide.

Thirteen-lined ground squirrel

Grey rock squirrel

The rather pretty Columbian ground squirrel, recognizable by its rusty orange face and tawny legs, occurs in the northern Rockies, south to central Idaho, and in southwestern Montana. It may be found from low valleys to Alpine country but usually only on grassy slopes or forest openings. These noisy rodents normally live in colonies of various sizes and produce a high-pitched chirping alarm note when intruders approach. Hibernation and aestivation (late summer dormancy) occupy from seven to eight months of each year for these true hibernators regardless of their habitat's elevation.

Columbian ground squirrel

Richardson's ground squirrel—the common gopher of the northern prairies

Farther south in the Rockies, similar habitats are occupied by the Richardson's ground squirrel — the common *gopher* of the Canadian Prairies. This ground squirrel has a rather curious distribution — a plains animal in the north but occurs to elevations of over 12,000 feet in Rocky Mountain National Park, Colorado. This rather drab grey or buff colored squirrel has no spots or stripes. It reaches its southern limit of distribution in central Colorado, and is always found in open meadows. The more attractive golden mantled ground squirrel is found mostly in dry, semi-open Montane forests from Canada south to New Mexico. It has a coppery head and a broad white stripe bordered by black on each side of the back. Mantled ground squirrels often are mistaken for chipmunks. They are larger, however, and have no stripe on the side of their face. This enjoyable species is a frequent visitor at Rocky Mountain campgrounds.

Golden mantled ground squirrel

About five species of the energetic little chipmunk occur in this region, but only two are widespread. The casual observer will have considerable difficulty identifying the species while afield, but this is probably of little consequence. The smallest of the group, appropriately called the least chipmunk, occurs throughout the Rockies from shrubby valley bottoms to alpine meadows. It prefers brushy, semi-open habitats and, when running, carries its tail erect. The second most common chipmunk of the Rockies is the slightly larger yellow pine or northwestern chipmunk, found from north of Jasper to about the Wyoming-Colorado border. It prefers lower elevation forests of Douglas fir and ponderosa pine, although it also can be found upward into the

Chipmunk

Young chipmunks

Subalpine forest. Three other species of more restricted distribution in the Rockies are the red-tailed, uinta and the Colorado chipmunks. The red-tailed chipmunk occurs in southeastern British Columbia, extreme southwestern Alberta (Waterton Park), northeastern Idaho and western Montana. It is restricted ecologically to the Subalpine zone of coniferous forests. The Vinta chipmunk occurs from extreme southern Montana (Beartooth Mountains) to north-central Colorado in coniferous forests between 7,000 and 12,000 foot elevations. Last, the very similar Colorado chipmunk occurs in our region only in western and central Colorado and northern New Mexico where it typically inhabits the lower mountain slopes of open coniferous woodland and broken rock.

Red squirrel

Tassel-eared squirrel

Red squirrel

Only one species of tree squirrel is common throughout the Rockies: the familiar bushy-tailed pine or red squirrel. It ranges across North America in the north, and south in the Rockies to southern New Mexico. The presence of these unstriped squirrels will be readily evident from their unmistakable chattering and their heaps of cone scales. These squirrels occupy coniferous forests at all elevations. One other tree squirrel — the very distinctive tassel-eared squirrel — is readily recognized by its prominent ear tufts and white tail among the foothills of lower mountains from the southern Rockies of Colorado to New Mexico.

The elusive northern flying squirrel, being nocturnal, is rarely seen but occurs south in the Rockies to southwestern Wyoming and northern Utah. It may occur also in northwestern Colorado, but this has not yet been established. These adept gliders of the deep woods are most likely to be encountered scurrying across cabin or tent roofs at night, a truly unique experience for the mountain camper.

Flying squirrel

Finally, the prairie dogs, considered by many to be strictly plains animals, do enter the mountain region. In particular, Gunnison's and white-tailed prairie dogs may be found in high valleys and mountain parks from extreme southern Montana to New Mexico and Utah. Yellowish animals, slightly smaller than a domestic cat, they are to be seen sitting upright beside their prominent burrow in open country. In Colorado, Gunnison's prairie dog ranges upward in the mountains to the 12,000 foot level.

Prairie dogs in their typical sitting-upright position

MANY WAYS OF LIFE

The squirrel family has probably been as successful as any group of mammals in colonizing and adapting to a variety of habitats and environmental conditions. In the Rockies, family members occupy grassland, shrubland, parkland, dense forest, Alpine and rockslide habitats. Included are hibernators and non-hibernators, diurnally and nocturnally active species, and examples of semi-fossorial, aboreal and volant ways of life.

No members of this group turn white in winter. Most hibernate, making them unavailable as winter food for predators. A few inhabit the treetops where a white coat would be disadvantageous. The tree squirrels and chipmunks gather and store food for the long mountain winter, while the marmots, ground squirrels and prairie dogs just fatten themselves, then hibernate.

Prairie dog fattens up by nearly constant eating before fall hibernation

The marmots, prairie dogs, ground squirrels and chipmunks all rely on burrows in the ground to escape danger, to hibernate, and to rear their young. These are perhaps best described as *semi-fossorial* species, reserving the word *fossorial* for such subterranean denizens as the moles and pocket gophers which not only show strong physical adaptations for underground life, but also obtain their food underground and only rarely venture above the soil surface.

Chipmunk burrows are usually well hidden beneath rocks or tangled brush, so very few have ever been dug up by naturalists. Some have side tunnels and accessory chambers; most consist of a single entrance leading to a single, unbranched tunnel which slopes gradually to a depth of one and one half to two feet. At the end of the tunnel is a nest chamber about six inches in diameter.

Full cheek pouches on chipmunk

The chipmunks also possess pouches on the inside of their cheeks in which they transport food to their dens. When cheeks are well filled with berries or seeds, the animal has a comical appearance, as though suffering from a severe case of mumps. The other burrowers — marmots, prairie dogs and ground

Prairie dog town

Hoary marmots

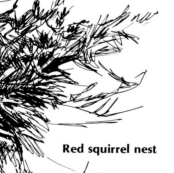

Red squirrel nest

Red squirrel

squirrels — are usually found in open country, often in groups or colonies, seldom straying far from the protection of their underground hideaways. Most of their food, which is almost entirely vegetable material, is gathered nearby. Without the brushy cover of the chipmunks, they are more vulnerable to the attacks of airborne predators such as hawks and eagles.

Burrows of the yellow-bellied and hoary marmots are almost invariably in rocky places, and often right among large rockslides or talus slopes. Because of this they are difficult to excavate and little studied. Many ground squirrels make elaborate subterranean chambers which are used year after year, each season seeing additions to and repairs of these long established home sites. None is more remarkable than the elaborate tunnels of the prairie dog, the entrances of which are protected from flooding by a mound of earth a foot or more in height. The abrupt holes plunge almost directly downward to a depth of ten feet or more, then continue horizontally or slightly upward. From this lateral tunnel short branches terminate in rounded nest chambers. A few feet within the burrow mouth is often a short side-passage where the retreating prairie dog may rest and turn to bark and scold at the intruder or return cautiously to the entrance to survey his domain.

The widespread red or spruce squirrels have taken to the trees to escape enemies and to obtain food. They have flexible fingers and sharp claws adapted to clutching the bark of trees, as well as a bushy tail which, it has been suggested, serves to break the force of inevitable falls when distances are miscalculated. These squirrels do not hibernate, and they usually build bulky nests of shredded bark, leaves, and grass, high in the branches of trees, or occasionally take over and improve an abandoned woodpecker cavity or hawk nest, or even a hole in the ground. Red squirrels store food for winter use, and their fondness for spruce, pine and fir cones has not been overrated. While small numbers of squirrels may inhabit woods lacking cone-bearing trees, and so subsist on mushrooms, nuts, and seeds, greatest numbers occupy coniferous forests. Here their populations are known to fluctuate markedly in response to success or failure of the cone crop.

In matters of food storage, none are as provident as the busy red squirrel who stores masses of cones and other fruits in scattered caches in the cool damp earth until such time as needed. Then they usually are moved one by one to a favorite feeding site where the refuse resulting from such feasts may form sizeable midden heaps. One midden in a dense spruce thicket was measured at twelve feet in diameter and nine feet deep.

Red squirrel

Mushrooms, too, are favorite squirrel food, and the observant mountain traveller may occasionally see them placed delicately in the fork of a branch to cure. They may be eaten directly or stored like cones for later dining. An intriguing question arises from the manner in which squirrels relocate their many hidden caches. Some now believe that the squirrel's sense of smell is most important to locate caches, although a few caches are never utilized. The squirrel, then, becomes an important aid to forest regeneration, ensuring that many cones (which contain the tree seeds) find their way into a suitable environment for seedling establishment.

The amazing flying squirrel has carried his arboreal adaptations one step further than his red cousin. This nocturnal squirrel has broad folds of skin which can be stretched out between front and hind legs on either side of the body, forming a parachute-like membrane. Throwing itself from a treetop or branch high in the air, it can glide easily, controlling its direction by varying the tension of its membranes and the slant of its tail. It can even turn in mid-air to avoid an obstacle. Before making contact with

Flying squirrel

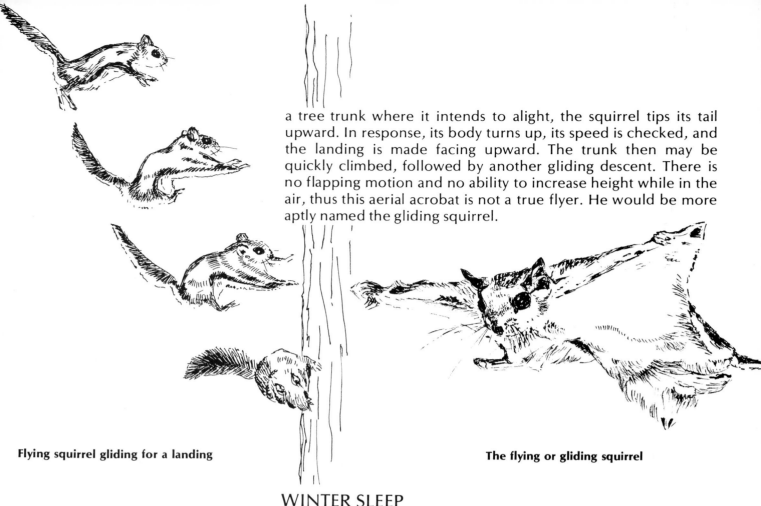

a tree trunk where it intends to alight, the squirrel tips its tail upward. In response, its body turns up, its speed is checked, and the landing is made facing upward. The trunk then may be quickly climbed, followed by another gliding descent. There is no flapping motion and no ability to increase height while in the air, thus this aerial acrobat is not a true flyer. He would be more aptly named the gliding squirrel.

Flying squirrel gliding for a landing

The flying or gliding squirrel

WINTER SLEEP

Hibernation has been mentioned briefly with reference to the bears and some members of the weasel family, but it is in the squirrel family, particularly the marmots and ground squirrels, where this phenomenon is most highly developed and has been most thoroughly studied. The period of dormancy may be very long and may include the late summer and fall as well as winter. Summer dormancy, more pronounced in hot, arid climates, is called *aestivation*, but differs little from hibernation.

In true hibernation, such as carried out by the Columbian, Richardson's and mantled ground squirrels, large amounts of body fat accumulate during the summer and serve to nourish the slumbering animal while hibernating. During dormancy the bodily functions are reduced to a minimum to conserve this vital energy source and ensure it will last the winter. In these ground squirrels the body temperature falls to within a few degrees of freezing, the heart rate slows from over 200 to as low as five per minute, and the breathing rate slows from nearly 200 inspirations to anywhere from one to four per minute. Not only does the heart beat slow down, but there is a decrease in the volume of blood in the blood vessels. A limb can be amputated from an animal that has been hibernating for some time and almost no bleeding results. Ground squirrels and marmots in true hibernation respond very slowly to handling or to noise and, if awakened at all, react dazedly.

Richardson's ground squirrel in hibernation

The chipmunks also spend winter in a subterranean retreat, but are probably not true hibernators because they store little body fat and prefer to pack a lunch. Up to a pint of nutritious seeds may be stored under the nest in the bottom of their burrow. There are two conflicting views on chipmunk hibernation. One is that they awaken periodically and eat some of their stored bounty; the other is that they do not hibernate until the food has been consumed. Thus true hibernation, if it exists in chipmunks, may be an emergency survival measure. Perhaps some hardy researchers willing to dig out chipmunk burrows in winter may be able to answer this intriguing question. Mantled ground squirrels also store a small amount of food and arouse periodically to consume it, but detailed studies have shown that hibernation reduces their food consumption to about 1% of what it would be for a ground squirrel in an active state in the winter.

Female chipmunk attending young in nest

Golden mantled ground squirrel hibernating

Young Columbian ground squirrels at burrow entrance

In the Rockies, both marmots and ground squirrels may have a very short period of above-ground activity, although this varies according to local climate. Most species emerge as early in spring as possible, usually March or April, and may even tunnel through the remains of winter snow to reach the sunshine. Males usually appear a week or two before females, but they also hibernate earlier. Adult males of some species, such as Richardson's ground squirrel are really only active above ground during the spring breeding period. In the northern part of this animal's range, males begin disappearing underground again after mid-May and are rarely seen after mid-June. Adult females have hibernated for the most part by mid July. Then it is the abundant young of the year which are seen above ground during late July and August, finally hibernating themselves by mid-September. Similar patterns are followed by most ground squirrels, chipmunks, and marmots, although the above ground period of activity may be longer. Chipmunks are the last to go under, braving the increasing cold of fall until late October or November.

Richardson's ground squirrel. Males usually come out of hibernation a week or two earlier than females

Chipmunks are the last to go underground

Porcupine

Beaver

Over-grown Rodents:

The Beaver and Porcupine

Two species, beaver and porcupine, are not closely related, but are discussed together here because, although both are true rodents, they are also misfits in the rodent world. Much larger than other rodents, each belongs to its own family: the family Castoridae in the case of the beaver, while the various North and South American porcupines belong to the family Erethizontidae. Despite their apparent lack of similarity with other rodents such as squirrels and the myriads of rats and mice, beaver and porcupine share one common rodent characteristic—they are possessors of well-developed, continuously growing upper and lower incisor teeth which they use for gnawing.

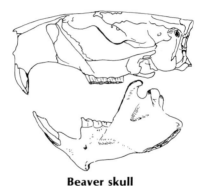

Beaver skull

Slow flowing stream dammed by beavers

Beaver

The large beaver with his big flattened tail is readily recognized by those who encounter him in the Rockies or elsewhere. In North America the beaver is one of the most wide-spread mammals, ranging from coast to coast and from Alaska to Mexico. Beaver occur throughout the Rocky Mountain region, generally not in high numbers because suitable habitats are restricted. They normally will be encountered at lower elevations where most of the lakes, marshes and slow flowing streams are located, and where deciduous trees and shrubs such as aspen and willow are most abundant. Rushing mountain streams, steep mountainsides and dense coniferous forests provide little in the way of beaver habitat.

Porcupine

The porcupine is almost as widespread as the beaver, although it is absent in the southern United States. Porcupines occur throughout the Rockies, but typical habitats are not easy to describe. Those who have searched for porkies will agree that "porcupines are where you find them," even in low shrubland, miles from the nearest tree. They are primarily forest dwellers, however, and are encountered at any elevation, although thinly distributed and seldom found in aggregations.

NATURE'S ENGINEERS

The beaver, largest of North American rodents, was greatly reduced by trapping in the western mountains in the late eighteen hundreds, but populations have recovered during the past 50 years. The most aquatic of rodents, the beaver is characterized by dense underfur (to keep the cold water away from his skin) and hind feet which are large and webbed. The beaver's eyes are set high on the head so that it can see while swimming and it is physiologically adapted for staying underwater for several minutes. Water is essential for beaver survival, and the animals are never found far from it, being awkward and slow on land and thus vulnerable to predation.

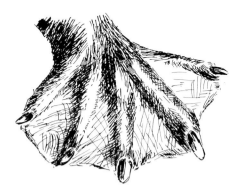
Large webbed hind foot of beaver

The beaver, largest and most aquatic of North America's rodents

...yet slow and cumbersome on land

Beaver habitat in the Rockies is usually along the slower flowing streams at middle and lower elevations, particularly where aspen and willow, their favorite foods, are abundant nearby. Streams must have sufficient flow so that the animal's pond does not dry up in winter, but not so much flow that dams and houses are damaged by spring runoff. Beavers adapt in several ways to survive cold mountain winters. First, being aquatic they live in an environment which never drops below freezing temperature.

Mother beaver's swimming lesson for junior

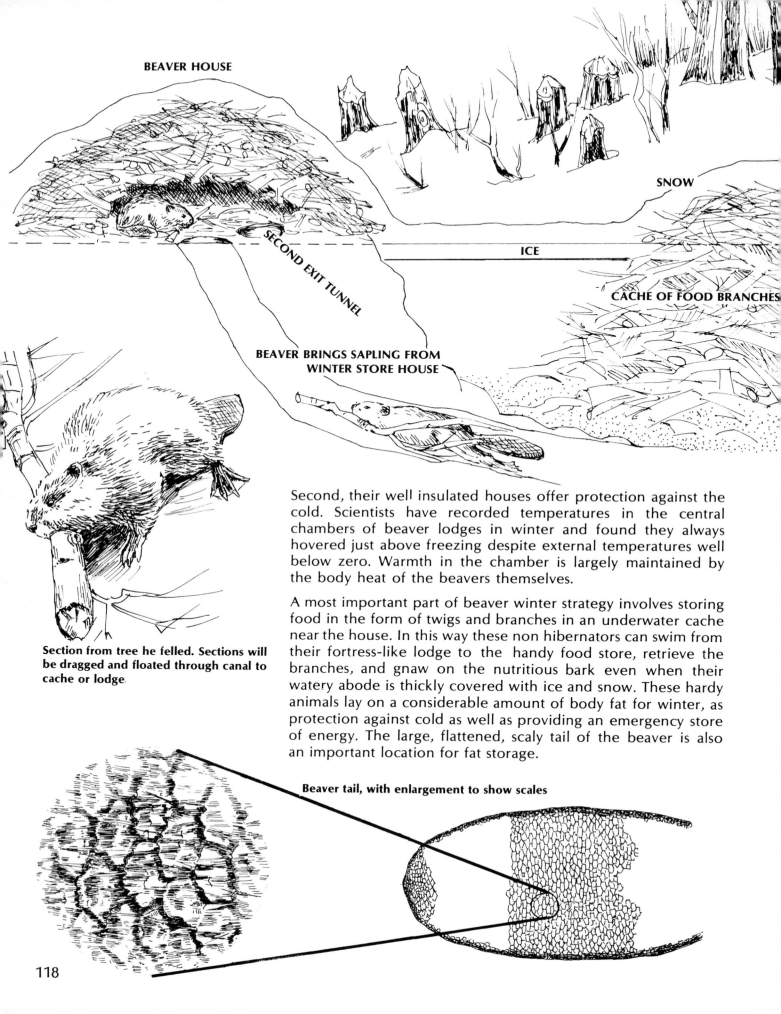

BEAVER HOUSE

SNOW

ICE

SECOND EXIT TUNNEL

CACHE OF FOOD BRANCHES

BEAVER BRINGS SAPLING FROM
WINTER STORE HOUSE

Section from tree he felled. Sections will
be dragged and floated through canal to
cache or lodge.

Second, their well insulated houses offer protection against the cold. Scientists have recorded temperatures in the central chambers of beaver lodges in winter and found they always hovered just above freezing despite external temperatures well below zero. Warmth in the chamber is largely maintained by the body heat of the beavers themselves.

A most important part of beaver winter strategy involves storing food in the form of twigs and branches in an underwater cache near the house. In this way these non hibernators can swim from their fortress-like lodge to the handy food store, retrieve the branches, and gnaw on the nutritious bark even when their watery abode is thickly covered with ice and snow. These hardy animals lay on a considerable amount of body fat for winter, as protection against cold as well as providing an emergency store of energy. The large, flattened, scaly tail of the beaver is also an important location for fat storage.

Beaver tail, with enlargement to show scales

118

Playful beaver kits

A beaver lodge usually contains a single family group: two adults, their yearling offspring, plus young of the current year—ten or twelve animals in all. When time for the next litter approaches, the yearlings, now almost two years of age, must leave the maternal lodge in search of their own territory. This way the local group does not outstrip its food supply too quickly, although this does eventually happen. The two-year-old animals usually disperse widely in search of suitable habitat, but passively avoid territories already occupied by other family groups. Scent mounds located near the edge of the beaver territory are believed an important method of relaying such information to these homeless waifs. These piles of mud are impregnated with castoreum from the castor glands and serve as warning KEEP OUT signs. Almost daily young and adults of both sexes deposit more mud and scent at the mound to advertise the occupied territory to transients (primarily two-year-olds) and to members of neighboring colonies. One important aspect of this spacing system is that transient animals appear voluntarily to avoid areas harboring scent mounds. This eliminates the need for active defense of territories which would result in harmful strife and needless loss of vital energy.

Beaver gnawings

Beaver lodge

Beaver dam and lodge in background

The long term cycle of beaver occupancy and abandonment of mountain habitats results in considerable landscape change and biotic diversity. The aquatic habitat created by beaver impoundments is highly attractive to waterfowl and muskrats, and except for natural and man-made lakes and parks, beaver-occupied valleys constitute the only habitat where these species occur in much of the Rocky Mountain area. After abandonment the dried ponds form most attractive mountain meadows. Even if one is not fortunate enough to see these busy creatures at work, it can be a fascinating adventure to search out and interpret the signs of former beaver activities in many a mountain valley.

Before discarding the chips beaver eats bark off. A 4 inch thick tree can be felled in 15 minutes

119

Porcupine in "raised quill" defense position

Hollow quill with small scales which act as tenacious barbs

RAMBLING PINCUSHION

The porcupine, also known as porky or quill pig, is a unique mammal requiring little description. This large, lumbering rodent is reputed to be armored with 30,000 quills, although it is not clear how this estimate was determined. It is the only quill-bearing North American mammal. The hollow quills are distributed from crown of the head to tip of the tail. They are yellowish white with sharp, shiny, dark tips. The sharp tips possess small scales which act as tenacious barbs once they are imbedded in flesh. Readers who have had the undesirable task of removing porcupine quills from the mouth of a family dog will know how firmly they can be imbedded. These quills have long been used by native people who prize them for their decorative value in beadwork.

Contrary to popular opinion, the porcupine cannot shoot its quills at a nearby object; its usual method of impaling an attacker is with a flick of the tail—because the quills are only loosely attached to the porcupine, they readily pull out when the sharp, barbed ends are stuck in an attacker. But porcupines are not aggressive. Any animal running afoul of a porcupine does so as a result of its own aggression or curiosity. The slow moving porcupine may appear vulnerable to predation, but its quills—the mainstay of its defence system—usually are sufficient deterrent to would-be predators. When threatened the porcupine puts its unguarded snout between its forelegs, arches its back and rotates its body to keep its tail end towards the enemy. Vulnerable on the underside, the threatened animal instinctively lowers its centre of gravity and becomes hard to turn over. This defensive posture is accompanied by much clicking of teeth and grunting sounds. Despite its defences, the porcupine occasionally falls prey to various carnivores. The fisher is one of its more adept predators. Several persons have reported seeing the attack and kill. In all cases the arboreal fisher ran along the branch on which the porcupine was sitting, then swung to the underside of the branch, reaching up quickly to bite the unquilled underbelly and throat of the victim. A trapper recently reported that he had never caught a fisher that did not have some quills imbedded in its hide around its face and neck. A meal of porcupine is not without penalties even to fishers.

Porcupine going into defense position

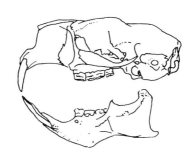

Porcupine skull

The hardy porcupine is active all year, neither hibernating nor storing food for winter, seldom even resorting to protective dens. In its forested habitat the dinner table is constantly set and much of the animal's activity involves eating. For this the porky is well-endowed with large, powerful, incisor teeth that have a yellowish layer of hard enamel on the front, and a thicker layer of white dentine behind. Because the dentine wears down faster than the enamel, the chisel shaped teeth are always sharp. They grow outward constantly from the root, and remain admirably adapted for cutting bark and wood.

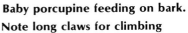

Baby porcupine feeding on bark. Note long claws for climbing

In the Rockies the porcupine is primarily an animal of the forest, although sometimes it occurs in shrubland several miles from real trees. Another favorite haunt, particularly in winter, is the low, stunted krumholtz forest often found on windswept foothills or at timberline. The feeding habits of porcupines vary regionally depending on the availability of preferred foods, but coniferous trees are always of considerable importance. The porcupine is capable of causing considerable damage to forest plantations which has earned it a bad reputation among foresters. Favorite foods in the Rockies include the bark of pines, firs, larches, spruce and willow. In the foothills of southern Alberta porcupines show a fondness for stunted patches of limber pine which provide protective cover and an easily reached, energy-rich winter food. The bark of limber pine contains high fat levels during winter, a time when porcupine survival requires high energy food.

Porcupine feeding on coniferous tree

Cousins by the Dozens:
Rats and Mice

Deer mouse

The vast array of furry creatures commonly referred to as small mammals undoubtedly is bewildering to the non-scientific wild-life watcher. Many of the various species look very much alike, and are observed so seldom that most people gain little familiarity with them. Nevertheless, rats and mice are an extremely important part of Montane ecological systems. For the most part they are primary consumers, converting plant material into protein. Their combined weight or amount of body tissue, biomass, on an acre or square mile of habitat may be very great (greater than the combined weight of the more obvious hooved mammals, for example) and they are the dietary mainstay of many other birds, mammals and snakes.

The small mammals in this chapter fall into two basic groups: shrews, which belong to a larger grouping called the insectivores (insect-eaters) plus rats and mice, which fall into several families in that large group called rodents. Moles are also insectivores but do not occur in the Rockies.

Bushy-tailed wood rat

Shrew

More than 30 kinds of small mammals exist in or at the fringes of the Rocky Mountain region. The fringe species are almost all animals of the arid southwest, intermountain basins, or Great Plains, which extend into the southern and central parts of the Rockies in dry, non-forested valleys. Thus they occur broadly in the region, though they are not typically Rocky Mountain species. These include Merriam's shrew, the olive-backed, apache, silky and great basin pocket mice, Ord's kangaroo rat, the western harvest mouse, northern grasshopper mouse, canyon mouse, brush mouse, pinon mouse, rock mouse, white-throated and Mexican wood rats, and valley pocket gopher.
The typical Rocky Mountain small mammals are mostly species which are widespread in the northern Boreal Forest zone and extend varying distances southward in the mountains.

These more common mountain species include the masked, wandering, water and pygmy shrews, the northern pocket gopher, the deer and western jumping mice and the bushy-tailed wood rat. Furthermore the northern bog lemming, and the heather, red-backed, meadow, water, mountain, long-tailed and sage-brush voles as well as the largest vole, the muskrat, are found here.

Lemming

Water vole

DIMINUTIVE PREDATORS: THE SHREWS

Shrews are remarkable little creatures with a mouse-like shape and very dense, soft, velvety fur. Their eyes are small and their snouts long and pointed. These tiny animals have a remarkably high metabolic rate. They do not hibernate, and continually consume large quantities of food—about two-thirds or more of their own weight every day. They will die in only a few hours if deprived of food. Food of the masked shrew, for example, consists largely of insects and their larvae, earthworms, snails, and centipedes. Shrews are also known to attack and kill each other, and even to take small rodents much larger than themselves. Some species of shrews have a poisonous saliva which probably stuns and kills their prey. The shrews' voice is extremely high pitched, and they apparently have the ability to hear sounds above the range of the human ear. These highly energetic mammals are short-lived, very few surviving from one year to the next.

Masked shrew

Young shrews holding on to mother and each other

The water shrew is a most striking and remarkable animal, having a dark back with silvery-white underparts and broad hind feet fringed with short stiff bristles—an adaptation for swimming. These adept swimmers feed upon underwater insects, snails and small fish, and occasionally themselves fall prey to larger fish.

Shrew

123

Pocket gopher

SUPREME BURROWERS: THE POCKET GOPHER

In the Rockies, the northern pocket gopher shows the ultimate burrowing or fossorial adaptation. The body is shaped for burrowing, having a massive skull (for such a small animal), short muscular legs with heavy claws, and minute eyes and ears. Sight is a little-used sense for these underground denizens. The pocket gopher also has a short, almost naked tail and large fur-lined pouches on the outside of the cheeks. The pouches, or pockets, give rise to the name pocket gopher and are used to transport food. The food, roots and tubers from various plants, is almost entirely obtained underground. Some is cached in storage chambers in the burrows.

Burrows up to 275 feet long have been described. Where there are well developed soils in mountain valleys, pocket gopher signs should not be difficult to locate. These may be mounds of loose earth pushed up from the burrows or sinuous earth cores on the ground surface. These cores are about two inches in diameter, and are formed when the pocket gophers push earth into snow tunnels during the winter. During winter these industrious non-hibernators do some above ground feeding under the protective mantle of snow. The signs left by pocket gophers are often attributed to moles, but moles do not occur in the Rockies.

Earth cores, raised under snow by pocket gopher

THE PROLIFIC DEER MOUSE

The attractive little deer mice are among the most widely ranging and abundant North American mammals. They are highly adaptable, having colonized a great variety of habitats and evolved in the process into an amazing number of geographic forms or races.

White-footed or deer mice are active during all seasons. Their cup-shaped nests are made of shredded plant material and tucked away into all kinds of cracks and crannies including holes under fallen logs, stumps and rock piles. Old bird nests also may be used. They frequently resort to mountain cabins or invade the food supplies of campers, and it is in such situations that the Rocky Mountain visitor, flashlight in hand, is likely to catch a glimpse of these active creatures scurrying over his sleeping bag or across the cabin floor.

Mother deer mouse nursing litter

Deer mouse

This mouse is almost omnivorous, but plant material, particularly seeds, is preferred. Berries, grasses and insects also are taken, as well as just about anything edible that careless campers may leave lying about. As this writer can attest, these inquisitive, exploratory beasts are not above sampling the human ear lobe as well. To the uninitiated, their nosy night raids on provision boxes may sound like the work of much larger beasts.

The prolific deer mouse annually produces two to four or more broods, each consisting of two to eight young. The young are soon active and provide ample fare for an army of meat-eaters such as hawks, owls, weasels, marten and coyotes. Despite this incessant drain, surging fecundity ensures a continued supply of this adaptable mammal.

Bull snake eating deer mouse

Bushy-tailed pack rat in cabin

Nest of pack rat in cabin

NATIVE MOUNTAIN RAT: THE PACK RAT

North America's only native rats are wood rats, commonly called pack rats. The bushy-tailed wood rat is a beautiful, fluffy tailed animal found throughout the Rockies. The foul odor in mountain cabins long-inhabited by this species will be well known to those who frequent such haunts. The odor is caused by rat nests: large masses of plant material and other debris impregnated with urine and feces. Such nests may be among rock slides, in mine shafts, under stumps or in little used cabins, and are often re-used for many years. In colonies occupied for many years, the

Bushy-tailed wood rat at nest

accumulated mass of excrement becomes a hard black mass, not unlike dried tar. Those encountering it for the first time often think they have found some strange mineral.

The name *pack-rat* is a result of their annoying habit of carrying off all kinds of small articles from cabins and camps to hoard in the vicinity of their foul-smelling nests. They seem to be especially fond of bright metallic objects such as cutlery and sometimes replace these items with such trivial things as sticks, cones or stones.

The pack rat is active all year. Its diet is very broad, consisting of green and dried vegetation, mushrooms, fruits, seeds, insects and carrion. Dried vegetation is stored for winter use.

Meadow vole

MOUNTAIN MEADOW MICE: THE VOLES

The several species of meadow mice or voles occurring in the Rockies are, together, both widespread and abundant. Like deer mice, they provide an important food source for a variety of avian and mammalian predators. Most of the mountain voles are found in damp places, or at least where there is a fairly vigorous growth of ground vegetation. They prefer bogs, meadows, and streamsides. The several species look much alike, and only the experienced mammalogist can reliably identify them. These mice have a chunky build with ears more or less snuggled into rather long fur.

An important feature in the meadow vole's life is its runways in the grass. These little pathways cut through the grass usually radiate from a burrow, leading from one clump of bush to another. In these runways, too, the careful observer may find little piles of cut grass stems where these grass-eaters have been feeding—a good sign of the presence of voles. During winter voles in the Rockies live beneath the snow and build a nest on the ground surface. When the snow thaws in the spring, these globular nests constructed of dry grass with an entrance at one

Meadow mouse—its long hairless tail with scales and bristles helps in climbing the grain stalks

side may be observed. Sometimes too, spring will reveal rope-like cores of dirt and grass cuttings mixed together. This is material shoved into snow tunnels during the winter, similar to the dirt cores left by pocket gophers.

In spring most voles move to underground nests, although some build their globular summer nests in tangled stems of reeds or cattails over the surface of water and swim to and from the nest. The large water vole of the Rockies, at home in the aquatic environment, may even have some of its burrow entrances located beneath the water surface.

The voles are great storers of vegetative material for winter. These stores, which may become very large, are usually located underground, although some may be on the ground surface at the base of shrubs such as willows.

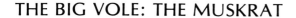

The harvest mouse weaves its nest with teeth and feet. Attached to high reeds the nest is made of grass and lined with soft materials

THE BIG VOLE: THE MUSKRAT

These widespread rodents, though not typically mountain animals, occur throughout the Rockies where suitable habitat exists. Their distribution is much the same as the beaver's. These overgrown voles are distinguished readily from the beaver, however, by their smaller size and cylindrical rat-like tail.

Muskrats are not particularly wary animals, and if you can locate occupied habitat you probably will see the unconcerned animals. The characteristic domicile of the muskrat in marshy areas is a house built of bullrush, cattail or other aquatic vegetation. It is usually in shallow water but some distance from shore, and thickly constructed as a defence against predators and winter cold, the largest reaching a height of three feet above the water. In deep, sluggish streams and backwaters flanked by high land, muskrats commonly live in bank burrows having entrances below water level.

Another structure indicating the presence of muskrats is the food shelter or eating house which may be built over a plunge hole at the edge of a marsh or on the ice in winter. During winter muskrats commonly push up various types of debris through a hole in the ice, forming a mass in which a cavity large enough for one animal is formed. This *push-up* becomes covered with snow which provides enough insulation to keep the plunge hole in the ice open. Muskrats also produce small scent posts, much as previously described for beavers, but smaller and less elaborate.

Muskrat feeding

Muskrat

The muskrat is an important fur-bearing animal in many areas. Sizeable harvests can be taken because of this rodent's high fecundity. Not to be outdone by its smaller cousins, the mice, the female muskrat produces two or three litters per year, each containing up to a dozen young.

Muskrat lodge of grass and soft marsh vegetation

LITTLE KANGAROOS: JUMPING MICE

These odd little mice are distinctive indeed. Outstanding characteristics are notably long hind legs, small forelimbs, and an exceptionally long tail. As with the kangaroo, the powerful hind limbs serve for jumping and the long tail for balance. These animals are thus said to be adapted for saltatorial or jumping locomotion. Such pretty mice also are distinguished readily from others by their dark back, yellowish-buff sides, and white underparts.

Another odd feature of jumping mice is that in spite of the animal's small size, and therefore its inability to store food reserves, it hibernates. It is active only from May or June to September. The winter retreat is a warm nest at the end of a burrow or burrows, and here the young are born. As is common with hibernating mammals only one litter per year is produced.

When alarmed these amazing little jumpers are capable of leaping a distance of six or eight feet. With such long successive leaps they are able to cover ground with remarkable speed. During normal foraging activity, however, their jumps are much less spectacular.

Jumping mouse nibbling on a wild cherry, one of its favorite foods

The mountain species, the western jumping mouse, is never found far from water although it shows no aquatic tendencies. It favors the thickets of shrub bordering meadows or streams, and the dense stands of wild herbaceous plants. Largely nocturnal, this fascinating little mouse is seldom seen by mountain travellers. Jumping mice do not make runways in the grass; however, the highly observant naturalist in suitable habitat may notice their little piles of grass stems similar to those left by meadow mice but usually longer. They also build a globular nest, either on the ground or at the end of a short burrow.

Flying Fur:
The Bats

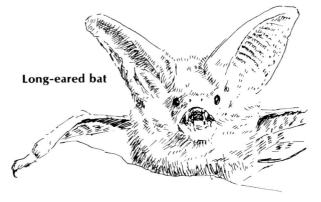

Little brown bats

Several species of bats may be encountered in the Rockies, although they are not particularly abundant there. Of the thirty-eight species occurring in North America, only six or seven are fairly widespread in the Rocky Mountain region. Bats are primarily southern mammals because their usual foods, insects and fruits, are more abundant all year in warm or tropical climates. Thus the total number of bats known to occur in Colorado, Montana and Alberta is, respectively, sixteen, thirteen and eight species, though not all occur in the mountains.

All bats in the Rocky Mountains are insect eaters. Because insects are not available in the winter, some species migrate southward while others hibernate even as far north as Canada. Those which hibernate relatively close to their summer feeding grounds are called cave bats since they usually choose caves or mine shafts for hibernation. These species usually form summer colonies in attics or other warm, dark, places. However, the bats which are summer visitors, leaving the Rockies entirely in winter, are often referred to as tree bats. They normally roost outdoors in trees or shrubs and are strong fliers. An example is the hoary bat.

Silver-haired bat

Long-eared bat

Bat species most commonly occurring among and along the flanks of the Rockies are: little brown, long-eared, silver haired, big brown, hoary, long legged, and Townsend's big-eared. A small brown bat at high elevations is most likely to be the little brown bat, although it occurs lower down, too. It has been recorded as high as the 11,000 foot elevation in Colorado. Most of the other species listed above occur in the middle and lower elevation forested slopes. Naturally, one cannot expect to be able to identify these aerial acrobats in flight.

Big brown bat

129

Bat wing—thin membrane is supported by arms, legs and tail

The bats are a most aberrant and unique group of mammals. While they are warm-blooded, have fur, and give birth to live young, they are not most people's conception of the typical cuddly mammal. The most striking bat feature, of course, is their mastery of true flight. They are the only mammals to have done so. Flight is made possible by a thin membrane supported by the arms, legs, and tail. The outer part of the so-called wing is supported by greatly enlarged finger bones. The large wing membranes and light body weight of bats provide for high aerodynamic capability. The largest Rocky Mountain species, the hoary bat, has a wingspan of about 15 inches but weighs merely 1.5 ounces. When at rest, bats hang upside down. Thus they are able to start flying by simply releasing their toe hold and spreading their wings.

The insect food of bats is captured while in flight. This includes mosquitoes, moths, and many other kinds. Where birds which feed on insects catch them in their bills, bats have a different technique: they scoop their tiny prey into the flight membrane which is temporarily folded into a pouch, then seize it with their teeth. The typically erratic flight you notice along a mountain trail at dusk is partially a result of this feeding activity.

Resting bats hang upside down

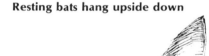

Little brown bat

Another fascinating adaptation of bats is the use of echo location or sonar to locate prey and to avoid obstacles. Most feeding is done at dusk or after dark. Bats' rather small eyes are of little use for feeding. To locate insects they emit rapid bursts of very high frequency sounds and pinpoint the source of the echoes. Thus their very sensitive and often very large ears are also of extreme importance. The sounds used for echo location are not audible to the human ear although bats also make other sounds which people can hear.

The little brown bat is a typical cave bat in the Rocky Mountain region as well as elsewhere. Summer colonies are often in attics or under siding, particularly in buildings near lakes. These summer colonies are made up of females which begin arriving about April and their single offspring to which they give birth about June. The young bat clings to its mother for the first several days even when she leaves the colony at dusk to feed. Later it is left behind while she hunts. The young can fly at about four or five weeks of age, and are mature by fall. Hibernation normally extends from September to April. Adult males are widely dispersed in the same general areas as the summer colonies of females.

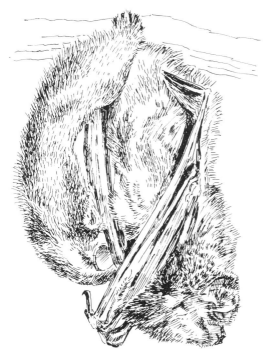

Hoary bat - mother with young

Bat colony

Year after year bats return to the same summer colony and winter cave. Both sexes hibernate in the same caves. In spring females leave the cave before males and again return to the summer colony.

Bats have few enemies other than the elements. They are known to perish in unseasonal storms or when caves become flooded. However, due to man's provision of buildings, mineshafts and other suitable habitats, numbers of the little brown bat and several other species are probably higher in the Rockies today than in pre-settlement times. It is unfortunate that man's effects on so many other mammals could not have been this positive.

Little brown bat resting

131

Drummers and Hooters: Game Birds

The tasty game birds of the Rockies have been as appreciated by hunters as those elsewhere but they also provide ample visual fare for the naturalist who is willing to seek them out in their particular habitats. The grouse and closely related ptarmigan belong to the familt *tetraonidae*. Seven kinds of grouse and three of ptarmigan exist in North America, but only three grouse (ruffed, blue, spruce) and one ptarmigan (white-tailed) occur fairly commonly in the Rockies.

The grouse are generally plump birds weighing from one to two pounds, and they have short, rounded wings. They are largely ground-dwellers and good runners, but capable of strong rapid bursts of flight for short distances. An explosion of grouse from almost underfoot can be startling indeed, but is also one of many rewards for the mountain hiker. A distinguishing feature of this family is that nostrils, legs and, in some cases, feet are covered with feathers. Grouse and their kin have short broad bills with the upper mandible curved downward. Grouse food is primarily vegetable matter, including green herbage, flowers, berries, seeds, buds, needles and twigs, while insects are important in the chicks' diet during their first weeks. Nests are always on the ground and the clutches of brown-hued eggs may vary from seven to fourteen. The nest is simply a shallow bowl in the ground, lined with whatever is at hand, plus feathers from the hen. Incubation lasts from three to four weeks. Only one brood is produced each year, but hens will often renest if the first clutch of eggs is destroyed early in incubation. Brood size usually dwindles rapidly in the first weeks after hatching from a variety of mortality causes. Broods often combine into larger flocks in late summer.

Blue grouse have short broad bills with upper mandible curved downward

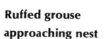

Ruffed grouse approaching nest

132

DISTRIBUTION AND HABITAT

The blue grouse is a bird of the mountainous west, found from the eastern foothills of the Rockies to the Pacific Coast and from the Yukon to New Mexico. In the Rockies, the hooter is most commonly found in the more open stands of Douglas fir and ponderosa pine, often on south-facing slopes. They are most abundant in British Columbia, Washington, Idaho and Montana. The spruce grouse, sometimes called fool hen because of their trusting nature, occurs in the Boreal Forest from Alaska to Nova Scotia and like many of the mammals discussed earlier exists southward in the dense Subalpine Forests of the Rockies into Idaho and southern Montana. The name Franklin's grouse cor-

Blue grouse

Spruce grouse—distinguishing features of family are feathers on nostrils and feet

rectly applies to the variety of spruce grouse found in the mountainous west. The wily ruffed grouse also occurs from coast to coast. In the Rockies it is confined mostly to lower elevations along streams and rivers where deciduous growth such as aspen is abundant. This species extends southward through western Wyoming into central Utah. It is referred to locally by many names including willow grouse and partridge.

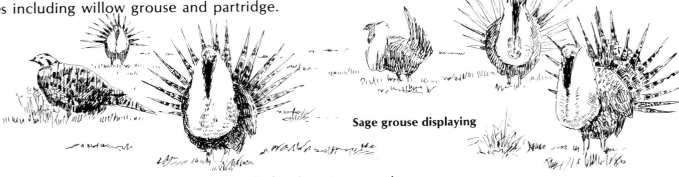

Sage grouse displaying

Two kinds of prairie grouse, the sharp-tailed (often incorrectly called prairie chicken, or just chicken) and sage grouse may be encountered locally in the Rockies. The sharp-tail occurs in dry grassy valleys and brushy habitats from Alaska south to Colorado. The large sage grouse, true to its name, is restricted to mature stands of sage brush. It is most abundant on the high plains to the east and west of the Rockies from Washington and Alberta south to southern Utah and Colorado, but it is distributed across the continental divide in suitable habitat from southwestern Montana to southwestern Colorado.

Sharp-tailed grouse

White-tailed ptarmigan

Of the ptarmigan species occurring in North America, the Rocky Mountain visitor is likely only to encounter the pigeon-sized white-tailed ptarmigan, which is confined to alplands of the western mountains from southern Alaska and Yukon south to northern New Mexico.

White-tailed ptarmigan

California quail

Ring-necked pheasant

Game birds of the family *Phasianidae* (quail, partridge and pheasants) are not common in the Rockies. The six species of native North American quail occur primarily to the south and west of the Rockies (except the bobwhite of the southeastern United States), although Gambel's quail may be encountered in bottomlands of sagebrush country in western Colorado and eastern Utah. Three introduced species—ringneck pheasant, gray (Hungarian) partridge, and chuker partridge—occur only spordically around the fringes of the Rockies.

Chukar partridge

Two species of the family *Columbidae* (pigeons and doves) may also be encountered in the region. The band-tailed pigeon, a bird more common on the Pacific Coast, nests in the mountains of Colorado and New Mexico but vacates these areas in winter. The more widespread and smaller mourning dove occurs at low elevations, primarily in agricultural areas north to British Columbia and Alberta.

Mourning dove
brooding its young

Band-tailed pigeons

134

The native wild turkey of North America, an important food source of the early cliff dwellers of Mesa Verde, occurs naturally in Colorado and New Mexico, primarily in semi-open forests of ponderosa pine and Douglas fir. It has been successfully introduced as far north as Alberta.

Wild Turkey

POMP AND CEREMONY

Grouse are fairly sedentary birds and although they may change habitats seasonally, they are not truly migratory. During the spring breeding season the male mountain grouse defends well-spaced territories from other males with an almost comic pomp and ceremony, display themselves vigorously to attract the opposite sex. Males inhabit the same territorial ground throughout life, and each species has a characteristic courtship display. The showy ruffed grouse advertises its territory by drumming from a fallen log or other elevated position. This muffled drumbeat often has wrongly been attributed to the beat of wings against a hollow log. Slow-motion photography and sound recordings have demonstrated, however, that the sound really is made by the bird cupping and rapidly beating its wings against the air. For the benefit of females attracted by drumming, the proud male then erects his ruff (thus the name ruffed) of dark feathers which surrounds his neck almost like an umbrella, bobs his head and ruffs back and forth, spreads his tail and struts about. Such a show!

Ruffed grouse advertising its territory by drumming its wings

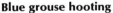

Blue grouse hooting

Blue grouse vocally advertise by hooting, usually from a high perch. This sound is achieved by expelling air from inflatable sacs on either side of the neck. At close range the head and neck of displaying blue grouse cocks are even more impressive than that of their drumming relatives. Bright orange combs stand above each eye, and the distended yellow nuchal sacs are each surrounded by a rosette of feathers with white bases and dark tips. The spruce grouse, by contrast, produces his territorial sound while aloft. This involves a short flight into the air followed by a fluttering descent during which the wings are beaten rapidly to produce a sound not unlike that of the ruffed grouse. The territorial male spruce grouse, true to family form, also struts about with bright red combs inflated, tail erect and spread.

THWARTING THE ELEMENTS

White-tailed ptarmigan in winter

Spruce grouse, like the blue grouse, largely live on conifer neddles in winter

The non-migratory grouse of our western mountains, like many of the mammals, must adapt to rather severe winter conditions. During the long winter in its alpland habitat, the ptarmigan finds it advantageous to don a completely white plumage. This provides excellent camouflage against predation, important for ground-dwelling species, and also aids in heat preservation. Blue, spruce and ruffed grouse, which retain a dark plumage all year, find winter safety by roosting either high in trees, or by burrowing comfortably under the soft mantle of snow. When perched in the open air, grouse, like many other birds increase the insulative value of their plumage by puffing out the feathers to make many small air spaces among them. Snow itself has excellent insulative properties, and birds buried in it may experience temperatures only slightly below freezing when the outside air temperature is well below zero.

But snow cover also has the disadvantage of covering much otherwise available food. Thus the winter feeding habits of grouse change markedly in winter and become very specialized. Blue and spruce grouse rely heavily upon the needles of coniferous trees and are specially adapted to digest these seemingly unpalatable items. It has been demonstrated that spruce grouse select needles of higher than average protein content in winter, and prefer older trees to young ones. Intensive studies of ptarmigan in Colorado show that various species of willow make up ninety percent of their diet in winter and spring. The ruffed grouse has his own winter specialty: aspen buds. For nearly half the year (late fall to spring) ruffed grouse are *florivorous*, that is they rely upon the flower buds of trees and shrubs, particularly aspen for their sustenance. From one perch a bird can break about a dozen of the highly nutritious buds, easily from the twig. Thus, when feeding on aspen buds, grouse are able to fill their crop quickly and dive into the security of a snow-burrow roost. This rapid feeding behavior has survival value because the main feeding period of the grouse is just before dark and coincides with the early foraging flights of such grouse predators as the great horned owl.

The ptarmigan has still other adaptations for snow and cold. In winter it grows fluffy stockings of feathers on its legs and feet, providing both insulation and miniature snowshoes with which to get about easily in soft snow. Ruffed grouse also have a sort of snowshoe, but instead of feathers they grow comblike fringes on the side of the toes each winter. These structures, it has been suggested, rather than being snowshoes are important for a strong grip on frozen, ice-covered branches. Future studies, hopefully, may be able to prove or disprove this interesting theory.

White-tailed ptarmigan—the highly feathered feet give protection from cold and enable bird to easily walk on surface of snow

GROUSE WATCHING

The best approach to grouse watching is a pleasant day's stroll through the appropriate habitats. In April and May, listen for hooting blue grouse on dry slopes and ridges covered with ponderosa pine or Douglas fir, and for drummers along the creeks below. Watch for droppings (like those of a chicken but slightly smaller) and feathers around drumming logs and dust baths. In winter, tracks and roosts in the snow and plant fragments dropped from trees are additional clues that grouse are about. Locating ptarmigan will require a diligent search of the Alpine Tundra, perhaps at Whistler Mountain in Jasper Park (accessible by tramway) at Logan Pass in Glacier Park Montana or at Rocky Mountain Park, Colorado.

White-tailed ptarmigan in alpine talus

White pelican

Waterfowl

Thoughts of waterfowl and shorebirds turn one's mind normally to our continent's vast coastlines or numerous prairie potholes, rather than to high peaks and waterfalls of the Rockies. But several outstanding wetlands occur in major valleys, and even the turbulent rivers support one or two avian species peculiarly adapted to them. The major marshes, such as Creston Valley, British Columbia; Red Rock Lakes, Montana, and Bear River, Utah, are as full of life as any on the prairies.

The Yellowstone-Teton area, a plateau some six to eight thousand feet above sea level circled by peaks rising another three to six thousand feet higher, can boost breeding populations of white pelicans, trumpeter swans, sandhill cranes, Canada

Canada geese and coots

Sandhill crane

geese, and California gulls, as well as a host of other marsh and water birds. The shimmering silver reflection of many lakes, large and small, and the calm, yellow-brown expanse of wide, warm rivers harbor an abundance of birds. Cormorants, Caspian tern, common loon, harlequin duck, willet, avocet, solitary sandpiper, shoveller, sora rail, great blue heron, and others earn distinction on a day's list because they are either rare or rarely seen. Of more common occurrence are coots, ruddy duck, pintail, green-

Pintail ducks

Blue-winged teal

Scaup duck

Eared grebe on floating nest

Buffleheads flying . . . swimming

winged and blue-winged teal, scaup, eared grebe, bufflehead, red-winged and yellow-headed blackbird, kingfisher, yellow-throat, tule wren, Wilson snipe, Wilson phalarope, and the inland waters constant companions: dipper, killdeer, and spotted sandpiper.

Yellow-headed blackbird

Such an abundance of waterfowl high in the mountains seems amazing indeed. The apparent cause of this unusual spectacle is the abundance of warm, shallow, waters which promote production of aquatic food in both streams and lakes.

Whistling swans

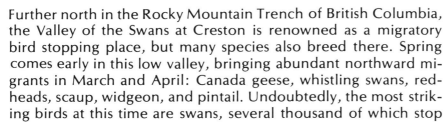

Redhead

Further north in the Rocky Mountain Trench of British Columbia, the Valley of the Swans at Creston is renowned as a migratory bird stopping place, but many species also breed there. Spring comes early in this low valley, bringing abundant northward migrants in March and April: Canada geese, whistling swans, redheads, scaup, widgeon, and pintail. Undoubtedly, the most striking birds at this time are swans, several thousand of which stop

Mallard hen and brood

Great blue heronry

temporarily enroute to their Arctic nesting grounds. In May, mallard and teal seek out nesting sites on the edges of marshes and dykes, and wood ducks and hooded merganzers search for holes in trees or nest boxes along the river banks. Here, too, many great blue herons congregate in their noisy rookeries, and red-necked and pied-billed grebes build floating nests among the reeds.

Marshes such as these present a unique opportunity for thousands of people to observe marsh and water wildlife in a spectacular mountain setting.

Wood duck

SAGA OF THE TRUMPETER

The trumpeter swan, largest of all waterfowl, was once very widespread in North America, but by 1900 was close to extinction. Swan skins and quills were valuable items of trade during the late 18th and early 19th centuries, and the Hudson's Bay Company sold some 108 thousand skins in London between 1823 and 1880. Soon, only remnant populations remained in Alaska and a wild part of the Rockies near Yellowstone.

Trumpeters, which weigh up to 25 pounds, made a remarkable comeback in the Yellowstone Park region after the United States Fish and Wildlife Service established the Red Rock Lakes National Wildlife Refuge in 1935. Under strict protection afforded by the Park and Refuge, the remnant population increased from less than 100 to more than 600 by the mid 1950s. These birds spend the entire year among the mountains, aided by thermal springs which provide some open water all winter.

Swans pair for life, but if one of the pair dies the survivor may take another mate. Pairing does not occur until the birds are about three years old, and initial nesting not until the fourth, fifth or sixth year. Trumpeters in the Rockies prefer muskrat houses on which to place their nests, although nest mounds resembling haycocks are sometimes constructed in shallow water. Nesting swans are jealous of their territories and claim large areas for nesting and raising their young. The clutch of five or six eggs is incubated for 32 or 33 days, but in some years as many as 50 per cent of eggs fail to hatch. On the average only two or three young or cygnets from each clutch survive to fly in the fall. Swans are long-lived, however, and this is sufficient to maintain the population, and to even allow for some increase.

In the Yellowstone region the number of trumpeter swans increased about 10 per cent each year for twenty or so years after protection began in 1935. The wide-ranging population of 97 swans counted in 1934 grew to 279 by 1944, and to 642 by 1954. After that, numbers leveled off and even declined slightly because the available habitat became full and would accommodate no more breeding territories.

Trumpeter swan

Swans from Red Rock lakes have now been introduced into several parts of their former range, so survival of a species once considered on its way to certain extinction now seem assured.

COLD-WATER DUCKS

Away from the marshy habitats and large lakes of the valley bottoms, one may still encounter two very hardy ducks in fast-flowing rivers, in beaver ponds, and in small cold lakes of the forested mountain slopes. These are the harlequin and Barrow's goldeneye. Both are diving ducks which spend the winter on the seacoast, but which find mountain seclusion to their liking during the nesting season.

A fairly large black and white duck. Barrow's goldeneye prefers small lakes and ponds where woods crowd to the water's edge. Male Barrow's can easily be differentiated from its cousin the common goldeneye by its crescent shaped, rather than circular,

Common goldeneye

Barrow's goldeneye

141

Barrow's goldeneye downies

Male harlequin

white marking in front of the eye. This is one of the few kinds of ducks which usually nests in hollow trees or stumps, perhaps a woodpecker hole enlarged by time and decay. The nest site may be close to or up to a mile away from the nearest water body. The pale green eggs are laid on dried wood and debris in the bottom of the nesting cavity to which the female adds a small amount of down each day until a rim is formed which helps to insulate the eggs. An occupied nest cavity often can be identified by bits of down adhering to its entrance. Soon after hatching the black and white downy young must tumble to the ground below and follow their mother to the nearest water where they soon begin feeding on insects, larvae, and pondweeds.

The courtship rituals of Barrow's goldeneye are among the most elaborate between ducks and include a formalized posturing in which the plumage, and in some cases the feet, are displayed. During these ceremonious displays, which take place in winter and early spring on the seacoast, a male will bow a number of times in front of the female, then stretch its neck upward to its full extent, showing off the iridescent violet head above the snow white neck and chest. Upon arrival in the mountains in spring, most of these ducks already will be mated pairs. Actual mating takes place in the general area of nesting but the males disperse again before hatching, leaving the care of their offspring entirely to the females.

Harlequin ducks

The harlequin is a slightly smaller duck, the male marked showily with white spots and crescents on a dark blue head and with conspicuous chestnut-red flanks. The female is smaller and drab by comparison, marked only with a small white spot on the face.

The cold waters of fast-flowing mountain streams are usual haunts of this diver, but lakes also are frequented. These colorful and agile ducks are at ease in the most turbulent water, where they dive to the bottom to feed on insect larvae or snails. Since such habitats do not produce much duck food, harlequins are dispersed thinly over the mountain region. But encountering this small sea duck in the seemingly inappropriate surroundings of tumbling stream, fern-decked rocks and overhanging forest is a reward indeed.

Little is known about the harlequin's biology and few nests have ever been found. But nesting is normally on the ground, often in dense shrubs or a recess among rocks. There are unconfirmed reports that this duck also nests in hollow trees.

UNDERWATER WALKER

Certainly one of the most characteristic, if not abundant, smaller birds of our western mountains is the remarkable dipper, or water ouzel. Four related dippers occur in Europe and Asia, but only one member of the family is found in North America. Our dipper is a true westerner, found along turbulent streams from Yukon to Mexico and Central America.

Dipper

The dipper is plain but unmistakeable. A bird slightly smaller than a robin, slate blue with no pattern anywhere, short tail, and found along mountain streams, is bound to be the lively dipper. The name is derived from the habit of dipping the body up and down by bending the legs, a frequent behaviorism. While there is some local migration southward and to lower elevations, dippers may be found throughout their range year-round, even in the north where fast currents or thermal springs provide small areas of open water.

Closely observed, a dipper does not appear particularly aquatic in its adaptations, but its dependence upon streams and some-times mountain lakes is no less strong than that of fish beneath the surface. The nest, a globular mass up to a foot in diameter, is often located behind a waterfall or in rock crevices in the spray zone of cascading streams. Man-made bridges also may be used.

In its feeding activity, the dipper is undaunted by icy streams, flying through foam and spray and actually swimming under-water, propelled by its wings. Where swimming is not sufficient, its bag of tricks includes walking on the bottom, a feat no other bird can do. The dipper's staple diet is aquatic insects and their larval stages, but small fish and fish eggs also are eaten. Some fishermen have expressed concern over its possible consumption of the eggs and fry of sport fish, but this is a small matter and aptly put into prespective by the eminent ornithologist James Munro:

> Perhaps food habits, good and bad, are trivial matters, to be set aside in such accounting; for in golden coin, minted for no material usage, the dipper pays full well through sum-mer and winter in song that is truly golden and a delight to all who hear it.

Belted kingfisher

KING OF THE FISHERMEN

A specialist indeed is the kingfisher, like the dipper, never found far from waters providing his fishy fare. The kingfisher family contains no less than 87 species distributed world-wide, but the only one we encounter in the Rockies north of Mexico is the belted kingfisher. This is a generally blue bird about a foot long, having a blue crest, disproportionately large bill, and white underparts with a large dark blue band across the chest. Its presence is usually made known by a harsh rattle of notes familiar to many an angler plying the same water.

Fairly solitary and widely dispersed, each kingfisher has its favorite perches from which it dives headlong into the water for small fish or, occasionally, frogs or large insects. Sometimes it hovers in the air before diving.

The kingfisher's nest is as unusual as the bird itself. Selecting a steep bank, usually of clay, both sexes engage in digging a tunnel up to six or seven feet long, ordinarily near the top of the bank. The eggs are laid on the bare floor of the chamber at the end of the tunnel. A section of lake or river is maintained as home territory for the exclusive use of one pair during the nesting season. For the first few weeks the parents feed the young with partly digested fish, later with small, whole fish.

Kingfishers are summer residents only in most of the Rockies, vacating the area for warmer climates in winter.

Young belted kingfisher waiting for food

Aerial Predators: Hawks and Owls

The two groups of birds known commonly as hawks and owls are adapted magnificently to a predatory way of life. For this reason alone they have suffered great losses at the hand of mankind. Adding insult to injury, many of their populations have been unwittingly decimated through man's indiscriminate use of various chemicals to protect crops and forests. There are hopeful signs, however, that these outdated attitudes and activities are changing.

Both groups of birds are characterized by short, sturdy, strongly hooked bills for tearing flesh, and by strong feet equipped with large, sharp, curved talons for catching and holding their prey. Both fill the necessary ecological niche of predators, or secondary consumers, the owls by night and the hawks by day. True to nature's strategy of filling all available niches through the process of evolution and adaptation, the remarkable owls are able to make use of a food resource not available to the daytime hunting hawks.

The owls by night . . .   **the hawks by day**

The predatory group known commonly as hawks is usually subdivided into *accipiters, buteos,* and *falcons.* The accipiters have fairly short rounded wings and long tails. They are largely woodland birds, seldom seen soaring in open country. The typical flight is several short quick wingbeats and a glide. Examples inhabiting our mountain woodlands are the Cooper's and sharp-shinned hawks, plus the larger goshawk.

Sharp-shinned hawk with young at nest

Red-tailed hawk plucking bird

Ferruginous hawk landing with prey at nest

The buteos are mostly large soaring hawks of fairly open country. They have broad wings, broad rounded tails, and typically soar high overhead in wide circles. Several species have light and dark phases, and this, together with immature and adult plumage colorations, makes them a particularly confusing group for the novice to identify. The typical, widespread buteo of the Rockies is the red-tailed hawk, but others such as Swainson's or ferruginous hawks can be found in particular habitats.

Falcons are the slim, fast-flying group beloved for centuries by devotees of the fascinating sport of falconry. They vary in size from the diminutive kestrel (often wrongly called sparrow hawk) to the powerful gyrfalcon, but all have relatively long, pointed wings and long tails. The wing strokes are rapid, and several species commonly hover in one spot (although other hawks may sometimes do this, too). The slim wings are not built for soaring like those of the buteos. For the birder lucky enough to get a close-up view, the toothed upper bill of the falcons is a good identification feature. In the Rockies, the most commonly observed falcon is the pretty little kestrel; less common are the merlin (often labeled pigeon hawk), prairie falcon, and peregrine falcon.

Kestrel

Prairie falcon with prey for downy young

146

Marsh hawk bringing twigs to nest

Turkey vulture

Other hawks or hawk-like birds which may be encountered in the mountainous west include the marsh hawk, osprey, turkey vulture, and eagle. The long-winged marsh hawk or harrier, a mouser of the marshes and open country from grassland to alpine, does not have pointed wings like the falcons and is distinguished by a white rump patch. The osprey, a large eagle-like hawk with wingspan of four and a half to six feet, is the only large bird of prey which has virtually all white underparts. Its habit of hovering and then plunging into the water feet-first to capture fish will distinguish it from other raptors.

The turkey vulture with its six-foot wingspan might be confused only with eagles, but its small head, two-toned blackish wings, narrow tail, and habit of gliding with wings held above the horizontal should distinguish it. Of the two eagles, golden and bald, the former is the typical mountain species. The golden eagle in adult plumage, lacks the white head of its bald cousin, but the young of the two species may be confused. Generally, however, immature golden eagles can be recognized by a white tinge on the underside of the wings and base to the tail.

Adult bald eagle

Young great horned owls

While about a dozen kinds of owls occur within our region, only a few can be considered common or widespread. Those most likely to be encountered or heard are the great horned, great gray, boreal, pygmy, and saw-whet owls. The great horned and great gray will both be recognized by their large size, but should not be confused with one another, since the great gray has no

Young saw-whet owl at nest

Boreal owl

ear tuffs. The pygmy and saw-whet are both tiny owls (six to eight and a half inches long) but the saw-whet is slightly larger than the pygmy and has a streaked rather than spotted forehead. The slightly larger boreal owl, has spots on the forehead, too, but should not be confused with the much smaller pygmy owl.

Saw-whet owl

Nest of golden eagle with downy young

GOLDEN MOUNTAINEER

If any raptor can be considered characteristic of the Rockies, it is the magnificent golden eagle, even though it also occurs in Europe and Asia and almost across North America. This eagle is usually a cliff-nester and, while sparingly found in badlands of the Great Plains or cliffs of the Boreal Forest, it is most at home in the high mountains.

Average adult golden eagles weigh about eight to twelve pounds and have a wing span of six to seven feet. Despite myths of them carrying away young children, tests have shown they cannot fly off with more than an eight pound weight.

Time of nesting varies greatly with latitude, but mostly occurs in late March, April and May in the central Rockies. The nests are usually of sticks and lined with grasses, leaves and various plant materials. Nests may be used for many years, becoming very bulky as they are enlarged annually. Usually two buffy eggs, blotched with brown spots , are laid and incubated for about 40 days. Adult golden eagles are extremely wary and have seldom been observed or photographed on the nest. Usually by the time the weary naturalist arrives at the nest site the adults are mere specks in the distant sky.

Because of their reputation as killers of livestock and game animals, the food habits of golden eagles have been well studied. In the Alberta Rockies, it is known that 68 Columbian ground squirrels were brought to a single nestling in a ten week period. Detailed studies of eighteen nesting pairs of eagles in a Montana study area showed that jackrabbits and cottontails made up about 70 per cent of the food items brought to nests. Other prey included marmots, magpies, ground squirrels, deer fawns, and gray partridge. Surveys of 41 nests in Western Texas and New Mexico revealed that 90 percent of the prey items consisted of jackrabbits, cottontails, rock squirrels and prairie dogs. Predation on game animals and livestock has only been observed occasionally, but does occur. There are at least two well-documented accounts of golden eagles killing antelope weighing 70 to 80 pounds. One such kill in Alberta took twenty minutes, during which time the eagle stayed on its hapless victim's back. As cruel as nature's ways may seem, they are a necessary part of natural ecological systems. Other predators, too, respect the strength of these magnificent birds. In Banff National Park, a single golden eagle was seen to drive two coyotes away from the carcass of an elk killed previously by a grizzly bear.

Golden eagle brings home prey for eaglet

THE ADAPTABLE OSPREY

One raptorial bird which, while not abundant, is perhaps the best prospect for adding to the mountain birder's list, is the fish-eating specialist, the osprey. World-wide in distribution, and not particularly adapted to mountains, the fish hawk can be found predictably in several mountain areas where rivers and lakes provide its sustenance. Large and conspicuous, and used year after year, the nests are fairly well known to local residents and naturalists.

Osprey nest on top of power pole

Despite heavy losses due to pesticides in eastern North America, ospreys have proved to be remarkably adaptable, nesting on power poles and artificial nesting structures, or beside railroads and highways. Known nesting sites include Talbot Lake in Jasper National Park; Vermillion Lakes at Banff; Creston Valley, British Columbia; Red Rock Lakes, Wyoming; and Yellowstone Canyon in Yellowstone Park. As early as 1932, the biologist George Wright remarked upon the adaptability of the Yellowstone Canyon ospreys to human disturbance:

> Before visitors came to this place, it was a concentration point for ospreys, and there is no evidence that civilization has diminished their numbers. Throughout the summers of many centuries they have raised their young on pinnacle nests in Yellowstone Canyon. Crowds of eager-eyed tourists on the parapets, which in some instances are almost directly over the nests, do not disturb the sitting birds.

Peregrine falcons

Peregrine falcon with eggs

PLIGHT OF THE PEREGRINE

The noble peregrine, formerly almost world wide in distribution, has declined drastically in numbers in many parts of the world including the Rocky Mountains, largely a result of pesticide contamination in their environment. Falcons, like other species at the apex of a food chain, are very vulnerable to such contamination, which becomes concentrated at each step of the chain. For example, pesticides used on crops may be taken up by plants which are fed upon by insects, which are eaten in turn by insectivorous birds, the latter being preyed upon by the peregrine, in this case a tertiary consumer. At each step of the chain the concentration of such persistent chemicals as DDE is magnified, resulting in amounts 100 to 1,000 times greater in falcons and their eggs than in their prey. Even peregrines nesting in the far north may be contaminated by feeding on migratory insectivorous birds from the south. Pesticide contamination usually has resulted not in direct mortality, but rather in abnormal behavior in which the falcons eat their own eggs or lay infertile, thin-shelled eggs. The results, however, are just as deadly to the continuation of peregrine populations as if the birds were systematically destroyed by shooting.

Peregrine surveys in the Rocky Mountains from New Mexico to Alberta revealed that only one-third of the previously known nesting sites were still active in 1964. Ten years later, scarcely any of those were occupied. Given time, hopefully, the lightning-like swoops of this majestic bird may be seen again in suitable Rocky Mountain habitats. If not, this region permanently loses a significant part of its prized diversity.

Peregrine falcon eating its own eggs

Peregrine downies

REPRODUCTIVE STRATEGIES

True to form for the summit predators, most hawks produce relatively small egg clutches, and the adults are quite long-lived. Since they normally are not preyed upon themselves, populations can be maintained with a fairly low production of young. Most adult raptors do not aggressively defend the eggs, although their defence of young in the nest has resulted in many a human injury. Since the eggs cannot defend themselves, a variety of safe nesting places are chosen: the tops of tall trees (osprey, red-tail, bald eagle), cavities in tree trunks (kestrel, pygmy owl, saw-whet owl), ledges on high cliffs (golden eagle, prairie falcon, peregrine), high up in dense coniferous foliage (Cooper's, sharp-shinned hawks), in dense brush on the ground (marsh hawk, short-eared owl) to even underground burrows (burrowing owls).

Osprey with fish landing on nest

Two young of the ground-nesting short-eared owl

Different size and age of immature nestling hawks

An interesting nesting feature of many raptors is the young in the nest may vary greatly in size, indicating that all eggs did not hatch at approximately the same date. This happens because these species begin incubation when the first egg is laid, rather than after all the eggs are laid. Such strategy seems an adaptation to varying food supplies, which is important chiefly for those hawks and owls whose food supply of mice, lemmings or hares varies in cycles. Since the first hatched and largest young are most aggressive in the nest, they are fed first and, if food is scarce, the youngest one or two chicks in a clutch of three or four will starve. How does this constitute an adaptation? It seems as if all chicks in a clutch of three or four were hatched on the same day, and were of the same size, the limited food would be divided equally among them and all would die of starvation. When food is abundant all young will survive. With these birds, then, the normal size of clutch tends to be somewhat larger than the number of young which parents can raise in an average year, the extra egg or eggs becoming a reserve which can be used in good years. Again, nature's apparent harshness is also an integral part of its survival plan.

NIGHT HUNTERS

Since man does not share the owl's remarkable nocturnal adaptations, night dwelling owls will seldom be encountered by the Rocky Mountain visitor. Nevertheless, a camper who hears the deep "hoo" of the great horned owl or the whistled "ook" of the pygmy owl undoubtedly will be curious about the life and times of these birds.

The staple food of owls is smaller rodents, mainly mice, and especially those species also active at night. The larger great-horned owl, however, regularly takes snowshoe hares and grouse. Owls are greatly aided in the night raids by very soft, fluffy plumage which enables them to fly almost silently. In addition, their hearing and sight are developed to a remarkable degree. The horns of the great horned owl are probably only incidental to hearing, but owls do have enormous external ear openings. In some owls the two ears also vary in location and size of openings and in internal structure. These are adaptations for sound localization, since nocturnal predators, especially, are dependent on an accurate directional sensitivity to sound.

Great horned owl with snowshoe hare

Owls' eyes are most highly specialized also. The eyes are not only large but directed forward, giving more overlap and, consequently, a wider range of binocular vision than in any other birds. Binocular vision is important in judging size and distance of objects, factors of great importance to predators. Owls overcome their restricted lateral and backward vision by lightning-like movements of the head which can be turned almost completely backwards. The huge eyes of owls accommodate an extraordinary number of highly light-sensitive cells known as *rod cells,* allowing them to see in light so dim as to appear completely dark to the less sensitive human eye. On the basis of eye structure, then, an owl's capacity to see in dim light is probably about ten times that of the human eye.

While most owls hunt at night a few, like the snowy owl and hawk owl, do hunt in daylight or at dusk. Even night-hunting owls have excellent vision in daylight except when brought suddenly from darkness into strong light. But most prefer to rest by day and await the nocturnal ramblings of their furry prey.

Snowy owls—male bringing lemming to brooding female

Compulsive Woodchoppers: The Woodpeckers

Yellow-shafted flicker

Of the 22 species of Woodpeckers occurring in North America, about nine can be encountered in the Rockies, and several are rather common. One of the most abundant is the red-shafted flicker, distinguished by its red moustache. This is a western species which sometimes interbreeds with its close eastern relative, the yellow-shafted flicker in the Rocky Mountain region. Flickers prefer very open woodland, and spend more time foraging on the ground than do other woodpeckers.

Two sapsuckers, the yellow-bellied and Williamson's, occur in the region. Only the sapsuckers have yellow underparts and a broad white band on the closed wing. Williamson's can be distinguished from the yellow-bellied by its lack of a red cap. The yellow-bellied prefers woodlands in which deciduous species such as aspen or birch predominate, while the mountain dwelling Williamson's will usually be found in dry forests of Douglas fir and ponderosa pine.

Downy wookpecker on mullen

The similar hairy and downy woodpeckers, both occurring throughout forested areas of North America, are black and white birds, males having small red caps. They are best distinguished by size. The little downy, our smallest woodpecker, is six to seven inches long, while the hairy measures about eight to ten. The downy is found more commonly in poplar woods; the hairy prefers more mature woodlands, usually with some deciduous trees present.

Two kinds of three-toed woodpeckers—the black-backed and northern—may also be encountered, the northern more commonly in the mountains. Both are distinguished by only three toes rather than four as in the other woodpeckers, though this is a characteristic of little value for identification when in the field. Males of both have yellow crowns, but the species can be differentiated by the plain black back of the black-backed and the horizontally striped ladder-back of the northern. Both species prefer rather dense coniferous forest.

Nest hole of pileated woodpecker with young

Two rather distinctive but not abundant species complete our Rocky Mountain list. A true westerner found from southern British Columbia and Alberta to New Mexico, Lewis' woodpecker, is distinguished by a greenish-black back, gray chest, and rose-tinted abdomen. It prefers dry open valleys with well spaced, large trees such as cottonwoods. Whereas most woodpeckers are characterized by a flight pattern involving a few rapid strokes then a glide, producing an undulating pattern, Lewis' flies with steady wingbeats like a crow. The largest tree surgeon, the pileated woodpecker, is widely but thinly dispersed. Its large size, scarlet crest and white wing-patches in flight are sure identification features.

153

Male and female hairy woodpecker

WOODWORKING SPECIALISTS

The woodpeckers (family *Picidae*) are well named, because pecking wood is what they do best. And to accomplish this they have been endowed with several appropriate adaptations. The bill, of course, is fairly large, strong, and chisel-like—ideal for digging holes in either dead or living trees. In order to use the bill effectively, very strong neck muscles have developed, as has the very heavy skull needed to withstand the brain-rattling hammer of bill against tree. Woodpeckers move easily up and down vertical tree trunks, rough or smooth, everyday activity made easier by short legs with sharp claws (normally two toes in front and two behind, except three-toed woodpeckers, which have two in front and one behind) and very stiff tail feathers'shape and muscular control allow them to be used effectively as a prop. Woodpeckers are thus best adapted for feeding when in an upright position.

These woodpeckers feed primarily on insects and insect larvae, since these are the common food items in tree trunks, stumps, and windfalls. The slender woodpecker tongue is fitted with several backward-pointing barbs at its tip, and can be extended far beyond the tip of the bill to impale and withdraw larvae and grubs from holes and crevices. Special glands also keep the tongue's sensitive tip covered with a sticky secretion which aids in extracting insects from difficult hiding places.

Yel l ow-bellies sapsucker drills holes and sucks the sap that runs out

THE GOOD AND THE BAD

Woodpeckers in general destroy a host of harmful insects, and thus may be considered the forester's friend. These insects are normally obtained from cracks and crevices in the bark of living trees, or by chiseling holes into dead or dying ones. Some species, such as the flicker, are quite versatile feeders, taking berries and fruits as well as insects. But a favorite food of the flicker is ants, often obtained from the ground. One individual is known to have eaten 5,000 ants in a single meal. A few species including Lewis' woodpecker and the yellow-bellied sapsucker sometimes capture insects in flight.

On the debit side of the ledger, the sapsuckers usually prefer to make neat rows of little holes in living trees, generally in smooth-barked deciduous species. Such trees are visited periodically to lap up sap which has oozed into the holes along with any adhering insects. This drilling can be injurious to trees, allowing the entry of disease-causing fungi and insects. Thus they are not popular with orchardists and foresters.

HOME-PROVIDERS OF THE FOREST

A most important and beneficial habit of woodpeckers is providing tree-cavity homesites for many other kinds of wildlife, principally in aspen and birch but also in rotted trunks or stubs of dead conifers. Yellow-bellied sapsuckers and red-shafted flickers are common in aspen grovelands of the mountain region and provide the majority of such cavities.

Studies in interior British Columbia show the hearts of most aspen trees greater than eight inches in diameter are rotted and most contain one or more woodpecker holes. Here the sapsuckers usually cut through a greater thickness of sound wood (about two inches) to reach the rotted core than do flickers (about three-quarter inches). Sapsuckers make new nesting holes each year, and sapsucker tenement trees may contain five or more holes made in succeeding years. These are quite small holes (about one and a half inches round) and are used by only a few other small species of birds (tree swallows, chicadees, red-breasted nuthatches). Many useable holes remain empty in succeeding years.

Flicker nest holes are larger (two and a half to two and three-quarter inches) and usually are in great demand by other birds, including starlings, mountain bluebirds, kestrels, pygmy owls and bufflehead ducks. They are used also by flying squirrels. Competition for these nesting sites may be intense, particularly if starlings inhabit the area. Those near lakes and ponds are prized by the little bufflehead, and if time and rot have enlarged them, by Barrow's goldeneye as well. At one particularly attractive site in British Columbia, dead female buffleheads were found in the nest cavity four out of ten years, and in each case the nest was occupied by a female goldeneye which had presumably killed the bufflehead and taken over the site. In at least three of those years, the same goldeneye was involved, and in one year she hatched a joint clutch of her own eggs with those of her dead rival.

Size of holes and nest cavities is critical for nesting habits. Of tree-nesting ducks, only buffleheads can enter and use the unaltered cavities of flickers. Other cavity nesting ducks must depend on holes of the larger, pileated woodpecker, on natural cavities, or flicker holes enlarged by decay.

The woodpeckers certainly are benefactors of many other birds, at least at nesting time. Many a hole-nesting bird at mountain slope and valley could scarcely exist without their wood-cutting skills.

Woodpecker hole occupied by bluebirds

155

WHITE EGGS IN DARK HOLES

The eggs of wild birds are well known for their wide array of hues and various patterns of speckles and splotches. But those of a few groups like the woodpeckers are always white. The simple explanation seems that eggs laid in a dark hole are not in need of protective camouflage, so why go to the trouble of coloring them? Holes in trees are not completely safe nesting places because squirrels, magpies, jays, and weasels are known to rob them, but once the nesting site is discovered, protective coloration would be of little value.

Woodpeckers lay their eggs on the soft layer of wood fragments and litter that covers the floor of the nesting cavity and provides the only lining. Nest sanitation is very thorough. At a carefully observed nest of northern three-toed woodpeckers, the male was seen to remove the feces of the nestlings a total of sixteen times in about nine hours.

Red-shafted flicker

Red-shafted flicker with young

Raucous Rogues: The Corvids

The family *Corvidae*, as a group, contains several species not only typical of our western mountains and valleys but, because of their boldness and raucous behavior, frequently are observed by hikers and campers. These include the jays, magpie, raven, crow, and that true western mountaineer, Clark's nutcracker. Much more conspicuous and less secretive than many groups (except when nesting) the corvids are welcome and delightful visitors to many a mountain camp or highway viewpoint.

Common crow

There are four jays in the region: the unfearing gray or Canada jay of the Boreal Forest and subalpine woods south to New Mexico; the Steller's jay, a crested species restricted to the Pacific Coast and western mountains from British Columbia to Cental America; the scrub jay of the scrub oak country in the southwestern states; and the smaller and plainer pinyon jay of the arid pinyon pine-juniper zone from Montana and Idaho south to about the Mexico boundary.

The unmistakable magpie is a western bird in North America, occurring in dry mountain valleys, plateaus, and adjacent plains from Alaska and Yukon south into Nevada, Colorado, and Nebraska. The unique gray and black nutcracker, or Clark's crow, prefers semi-open forest near timberline from central British Columbia and west central Alberta south to Arizona and New Mexico. The most common corvid, the crow, needs little introduction. Found throughout North America except in the Arctic, it is more migratory than its relatives, vacating most of the Rocky Mountain region in the winter. The larger but no more colorful raven is primarily a northerner and westerner, occurring across the tundra and boreal regions, and south in the west into Mexico.

The family is not well known for its singing qualities—the calls of most species being best described as raucous. Males and females are very similar in appearance. Since these opportunistic birds will indeed feed on a very wide range of items, food habits of the group are best called omnivorous.

Young crows

Gray or Canada jay

CAMP ROBBERS AND RELATIVES

It has been aptly said that the gray jay has more names than a debt collector: whiskey jack, Canada jay, camp robber, moose-bird, meat-bird, and so on. Well known to hunters, campers and hikers for its fearlessness of man, it will readily take tidbits from the hand, or from anywhere else not adequately hidden. Scarcely has the sound of gun or axe died down, when their fluffy ghost-like forms appear to claim a share of the spoils, the lunch, or whatever is available. This habit, however, is believed to be a learned one.

Gray jay . . .
taking tidbits from the hand

Gray jay

Despite this bird's common occurrence, few nests have ever been found. This is not surprising because these seemingly delicate creatures lay and incubate their eggs in March. That may be springtime in the low valleys, but deep snow and even sub-zero temperatures are the order of the day in the north woods and subalpine heights. Another reason why few nests are found is their concealment in dense coniferous trees, plus the shy secre-tive behavior at nesting time of this otherwise bold and inquisi-tive bird. The nest's basic construction materials are twigs, moss and lichens and it contains a deep cup lined with feathers, animal hair, or a combination of these items. The sheltered location, deep warm lining, and faithful incubation by the female usually are sufficient to protect the eggs from the chills of late winter. Typical gray jay nests are eight to fourteen feet above the ground on the south or southwest side of a spruce and facing an opening of some kind, perhaps a beaver meadow or just a small space left by a fallen tree. But there is always enough clearing to allow the late winter sun to reach the nest and to give the birds a free pas-sage to come and go. Gray jays are known to be territorial, de-fending an area of about one-quarter square mile. This area is only defended against other members of the same species, which are generally attacked on sight. The nest itself is not defended against other species unless the young are attacked and produce an alarm call. Such distress calls provoke a violent reaction in the adults, literally flying in the face of the intruder and easily repelling such potential nest predators as Steller's jays or red squirrels.

A persistent activity of the gray jay is storing food, which they have been observed to do at all seasons. Insects are probably the most important food, but berries and carrion are taken, and there are authenic observations of jay predation on live mice. The method of storing food is probably unique among North American birds. Anything intended for storage is manipulated in the mouth into an oval wad, impregnated and coated externally with a thick saliva which sticks to anything it touches. This *bolus* is pushed into a crevice in the bark of a tree, among the needles of a conifer, under a tuft of lichen or similar place. It has the appearance of an object coated with shellac. It is not known how much of the food is recovered later, but there is no doubt that without its habit of compulsive storage the gray jay could not survive on a small territory in such a harsh environment.

The more boisterous blue Steller's jay (not to be confused with its eastern cousin, the blue jay) usually will not be found in the same dense spruce forests as the gray jay, but may be attracted to the same feeding places. At Cameron Lake in Waterton Lakes National Park, Alberta, Steller's and gray jays, as well as Clark's nutcracker, have been noted all searching for tidbits in the same campground. Steller's is normally found at lower elevations in more broken forest and is abundant westward to the Pacific Coast. This noisy jay is a busy-body of the woods, loudly proclaiming the presence of hunter, hiker, or furry predator to all within hearing range. Yet Steller's jay is known to do a little marauding itself, conducting nest robbing forays with a stealth befitting those it would scold.

Gray jay

Steller's jay

Clark's nutcracker

Clark's nutcracker and curious little chipmunk

MR. CLARK'S DISCOVERY

Should there be an avian emblem of our high western mountains, none would be more fitting in my estimation than the distinguished Clark's nutcracker. This subalpine inhabitant was discovered during the Lewis and Clark expedition to the northwest in the early eighteen hundreds and named after that expedition's co-leader. The term *nutcracker* evidently refers to its dexterity in opening cones and nuts to get at the seeds inside.

Little is known about the life history of this stout gray bird with long black bill and black with white patches. True to form for the corvids, nutcrackers are curious and noisy. The harsh grating calls, repeated two or three times, sound like "char-r-r" or "kra-a-a." The habitat preferred by this species is semi-open spruce forest just below timberline. The bulky nest is built in a tall coniferous tree, and nesting is in March and April, relatively early considering the high elevation of nutcracker habitat. Like the jays, these usually noisy birds are silent and furtive at nesting time.

Nutcracker

Seed of the cone-bearing trees is the usual and preferred food of Clark's crow, particularly in winter, and a good cone year is a time of plenty and successful reproduction. Cone crops are known to vary greatly, however, and in a poor year the birds may turn somewhat to other mountain foods, though many also disperse widely into valleys and out onto the plains. Occasional winter wanderings far from the normal range result in curiosity and speculation about the identity of strange newcomers. In the summer and fall, insects and berries are important to its diet. Carrion may attract them at times, and they are reported to occasionally rob the eggs of other birds. Despite such lapses from an otherwise model life, the raucous nutcracker is regarded affectionately by many a high-country traveller.

Full curl bighorn ram

Bighorn ewe and lamb

5

Mixed group of bighorn rams and ewes on winter range

Mixed group of bighorns on winter range

Bighorn rams . . . drinking

Bighorn with magpie standing by in hopes sheep attract park visitors to throw out food

Three bighorn rams survey countryside

Bighorn sheep along the Athabaska River

Artist Susan Im Baumgarten meets her subjects

8

MOUNTAIN GOAT
Oreamnos americanus

Vital Statistics:

	Billy	Nanny
Horned sex	Billy and nanny	
Birth weight	About 7 lbs.	
Adult weight	140-250 lbs.	100-210 lbs.
Adult shoulder height	40-44 in.	35-40 in.
Maximum lifespan	Not known	

Horns:

Male horns thicker at base and curve gradually near the tip. Nanny horns curve sharply at tip. Record horn length 12 in., but average about 9 in. for billies and 8 in. for nannies.

Reproduction:

Billies: Sexually mature at 1½ to 2½ years of age, but most breeding is by older males. Rutting period about November.

Nannies: Produce first young at about 3 years of age. Gestation period about 180 days.

Kids: One is usual, but up to 25 percent of births may be twins. Young born May-June.

Food:

Very variable food habits. Grasses, sedges, and herbs important in spring and summer, including kobresia, bluegrasses, wheatgrass, fescue, and clover. Woody browse eaten in winter includes willows, bear-berry, blueberries, Douglas fir, and alpine fir.

Habitat:

Mountain goats inhabit the most rugged mountain terrain, frequenting in winter cliffs too sheer to hold snow. They also forage alpine meadows and forests—all the way to sea level along the British Columbia coast.

Mountain goats searching for food where either wind has blown snow away or cliffs were too precipitous to hold snow

Mountain goat nannies and kid graze high meadow— note new short summer coat

Nanny with twin kids

11

Mother teaches kid the ropes

Goats at mineral lic[k]

Mixed group of nannies and kids on summer range

When danger approaches kid goes to nanny and rubs muzzles. She responds by hanging her head protectively over kid. Ears down is threat— in this case to photographer who was too close

BISON
Bison bison

Vital Statistics:

	Bull	Cow
Horned sex	Bull and cow	
Birth weight	No information	
Adult weight	900-1800 lbs.	750-1100 lbs.
Adult shoulder height	60-72 in.	52-60 in.
Maximum lifespan	Up to 40 years	

Horns:

Horns project laterally in the calves, then gradually turn upward, and finally inward at the tips in adult animals. Male horns larger than those of female.

Reproduction:

Bulls: Most reach sexual maturity at 2-3 years of age. Rutting period is July to September.

Cows: A few precocious cows conceive as yearlings. About half of the two-year-olds conceive (bear first young at about third birthday). All females sexually mature by 3½ years of age, but usually only produce about 2 calves every 3 years. Gestation period 270-300 days.

Calves: One is the rule. Mostly born from late April into June.

Food:

Grasses, sedges, and small herbs predominate. Staple foods include wheatgrasses, fescue, bluegrass, and brome.

Habitat:

The buffalo, now exterminated from the prairies, occupies aspen parkland, grassy benches and open coniferous forests.

Plains bison or buffalo

A test of strength . . . of perpetuation

15

Buffalo cow giving reassurance and protection to calf.

Herd of bison—a remnant of the millions that swarmed the prairies and Rocky Mountain foothills

The buffalo's thick winter fur and and great bulk enable him to withstand the worst winter blizzards 17

WAPITI
Cervus elaphus

Vital Statistics:

	Bull	Cow
Antlered sex	Bull only	
Birth weight	25-35 lbs.	
Adult weight	600-1100 lbs.	450-750 lbs.
Adult shoulder height	55-65 ins.	50-55 ins.
Maximum life span	12-14 yrs.	18-21 yrs.

Reproduction:

Bulls: Sexually mature at 1½ to 2½ years, but most breeding done by bulls 4 years old and older.

Cows: Up to 25 percent may breed as yearlings. Most cows do not conceive until 2½ years old.

Calves: One per birth is usual; twins occur rarely.

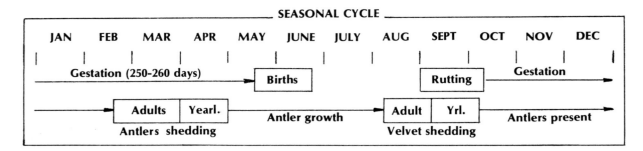

Food:

In summer the elk are primarily grazers, preferring blue grass, brome, wheatgrass, sedge, many forbs, mushrooms and horsetails. Winter fare is more opportunistic—browse of many shrubs and trees supplementing grasses that are revealed by pawing away snow.

Habitat:

Meadows, open prairie, parkland and forest.

Bull elk with attendant cow bugles to rivals that this is his area

Doe with new born twin calves. When the winter hasn't been too severe and winter and spring food has been in abundance over 50 percent of the does will give birth to twins

She licks fawns clean after birth

A rest from nursing! Fawn watches photographer

O.K. world—here I am!

Bucks in velvet

A prime buck

A forked buck basks in winter sun

The encounter—bucks lock antlers in test of strength

In winter the deer often 'yard' up—that is gather in small herds in good wintering areas. Here they trample down snow as a cattle yard to facilitate moving around to patches of browse. They are often reluctant to leave these areas even when overbrowsed. Cougars and wolves encountering these herds scatter them, therefore force deer into new feeding areas—often essential for their own survival.

WHITE-TAILED DEER
Odocoileus virginanus

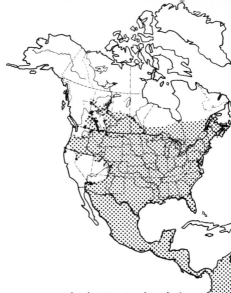

Vital Statistics:	Buck	Doe
Antlered sex	Buck only	
Birth weight	7½ lbs.	6 lbs.
Adult weight	150-300 lbs.	110-160 lbs.
Adult shoulder height	36-40 in.	35-36 in.
Maximum lifespan	12-15 yrs.	15-18 yrs.

Antlers:

Yearlings usually produce spike or two-point antlers, but up to 8 points recorded. Typical adults have 5 to 8 points on each antler.

Reproduction:

Bucks: Sexually mature as yearlings, but most breeding done by older bucks. Rutting period October-November.

Does: Small percentage may breed as fawns, but most not until yearling age. Gestation period 205-210 days.

Fawns: Yearlings usually bear a single fawn. Twinning is frequent in older does, while triplets are rare.

Food:

Mainly woody twigs (browse), but some grass, herbs, fruits and mushrooms in spring and summer. Common foods include aspen, rose, chokecherry, serviceberry and willows.

Habitat:

Prefer open edges of deciduous forests, glades, stream banks and in grassland and prairie areas frequent wooded draws during day, and forage open prairie at twilight.

White-tails prefer open woodlets and farm land and have entered the Rocky Mountain area through many of the river valleys. While the spotted fawns are difficult to differentiate from mule deer the brown and white tail in adults lacks the black tip of the mule deer

White-tail doe and fawn

Elegant young buck is lured into range as photographer imitates doe call during mating season

Buck clearly showing branching pattern of white-tail antlers plus forward sweeping main stem with tines branching off upward. Mule deer antlers keep forking

Doe in distress due to heavy snow tries to reach brush

PRONGHORN ANTELOPE
Antilocapra

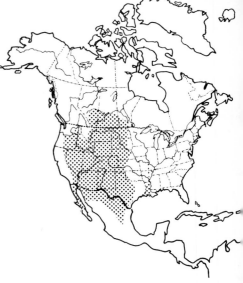

Buck   Doe

Vital Statistics:

Horned sex	Buck and doe	
Birth weight	4-5 lbs.	
Adult weight	110-160 lbs.	100-130 lbs.
Adult shoulder height	33-36 in.	32-35 in.
Maximum lifespan	10-12 yrs.	

Horns:

Both sexes have black horns with a forward prong and curved tips. Buck horns up to 20 in. long; those of female much smaller and often lacking. Sheaths shed in late fall.

Reproduction:

Bucks: Sexually mature as yearlings, but most breeding done by older bucks. Rutting period September-October.

Does: Conception rarely occurs in first autumn . Most yearling and older does conceive annually. Gestation period 230-240 days.

Fawns: Twins are the rule, singles and triplets occurring less commonly. Season of birth April-June.

Food:

Browse plants make up over half of the annual diet. Those include sagebrush, rabbitbrush, and winter fat. Grasses are important in spring, and a variety of herbs in summer.

Habitat:

The pronghorns are animals of the open plains, steppes, and foothills, seeking protection in coulees and river valleys.

Fleet of foot, the antelope's defence is alertness and speed

Pronghorn males have a branching horn which, unlike the other horned animals, is shed annually leaving the bony hair-covered stump to grow another horny outer cover

Pronghorn antelope enter the Rocky Mountain region through the dry valley extensions of the Great Plains

BLACK BEAR
Ursus americanus

Vital Statistics:

Weight:

Birth	½ lb.
Cubs (6 months)	20-30 lb.
Yearlings	40-60 lb.
Adult females	100-225 lb.
Adult males	250-400 lb.

Size:

Female height at shoulder	2-3 ft.
Total length	5 ft.
Male height at shoulder	2½-3 ft.
Total length	6 ft.
Adult tracks	about 7″ long
Adult droppings	under 2″ diameter

Reproduction:

One to four cubs are born in the den during late January or early February. Cubs weigh less than half a pound at birth, are weaned at five months, but don't become independent until after the first winter's denning with their mother. The sow chases the yearling cubs away before mating again. Therefore productive sows only breed every two years. Maturity is reached at 4-5 years.

Food:

Black bears are omnivorous—eating vegetation and animal matter with the latter being either freshly caught or more commonly rotting carrion. In spring after emerging from the winter den, they eat conifer needles and new grass shoots and seek out horsetails and berries as the season progresses. Garbage dumps are favorite feasting areas.

Habitat:

Blacks inhabit both coniferous and deciduous forests and associated openings from sea level to subalpine areas. Caves or hollows under stumps are favored denning sites which are occupied from October-December through to April.

Cubs scramble up trees at first sign of danger and mother may leave them there for several hours.

Both black bear cubs and adults can climb trees, therefore, if you are attacked, trees aren't a safe retreat

Opposite: Boar black bear.
Below and above: Sow brown black bear with one brown and one black cub.

Black bears are omnivorous and while the bulk of their diet consists of vegetation they are fond of meat—even well aged carcasses which they will stay around for many days.

Cub just out of den.

A mid-winter feed on frozen berries.

Playful black bears have often tempted people into thinking that they are tame—even park bears are basically wild and potentially dangerous.

Cinnamon-color-phase black bear resting in heights of ponderosa pine. Black bears come in many color phases including black, brown, cinnamon, yellow, white, and blue.

Black bears are good swimmers and readily take to water.

Bear steals supper from park garbage can.

Grizzly bear puts run on black bear at park garbage dump. Blacks have much better adapted to white man's civilization—existing in fairly large numbers throughout the west, while the grizzly has disappeared except for remnant populations protected in Yellowstone Park and the Canadian National Parks.

Bear trap—used to remove problem bears from park campsite.

GRIZZLY BEAR
Ursus arctos

Vital Statistics:

Weight:

Weight at birth	1½ lb.
Weight of cubs (6 months)	25-40 lb.
Weight of yearlings	65-90 lb.
Weight of adult females	250-350 lb.
Weight of adult males	350-800 lb.

Size:

Female height at shoulder	3-3½ ft.
Total length	5-6 ft.
Male height at shoulder	3-3½ ft.
Total length	6-7½ ft.
Adult tracks	about 10″ long
Adult droppings	over 2″ diameter

Reproduction:

Like the blacks, and most other mammals for that matter, grizzly sows cannot conceive while lactating so generally only have cubs every second year. Sexual maturity is attained at 6 years. The average litter size is 2 but 1-4 is the range.

Food:

Grizzlies are omnivorous but predominately eat vegetation—succulent grasses, skunk cabbage, licorice root, etc. Ground squirrels and marmots are occasionally dug from their burrows and spawning salmon are priority foods when and where available. Winter and road kills are also utilized along with human garbage.

Habitat:

While preferring open areas, the grizzly has been so reduced in numbers that it has been pushed into areas remote from man. These are largely alpine and subalpine meadows of the mountain parks or wilderness areas. After emerging from the winter den, lower areas are first to yield succulent vegetation. Winter dens are dug rather than natural hollows as used by the blacks.

Grizzly bear—a picture of power

The grizzly is a wilderness seeker—preferring lonely alpine meadows and remote river valleys. The near 1,000-pound adults can easily outrun a human and the only safe retreat is standing still in hopes an angered bear won't complete his charge, or quickly climbing a tree. The best defense is to make lots of noise while hiking so the bears can avoid you

The grizzly is best distinguished from the black bear by the former's protruding shoulder hump and its long claws which are used for digging

An unfinished road-killed carcass offers many meals—between feeds grizzly will bury carcass or sleep on guard nearby.

The grizzly bear is predominantly a vegetarian but readily accepts—probably even prefers—meat when it is easily available. Grizzlies congregate on salmon spawning rivers and winter or road kills and, if available, will readily stoop to scavenging human garbage dumps.

OPEN OTHER END

COUGAR
Felis concolor

Vital Statistics:

Weight (pounds):	
At birth	1
Adult male	160 (125 - 200)
Adult female	100 (80 - 135)
Total length:	
Adult male	6½ - 9 ft.
Adult female	6 - 7 ft.
Shoulder height:	
Adult male	26 - 32 in.
Adult female	22 - 28 in.

Reproduction:

Cougars can mate and subsequently give birth at any season but most young seem to be born in January and February. One to five kittens, with three being the average, are born after a 90 day gestation period. The young become independent at one and one-third to two years and reach sexual maturity at two to three years.

Food:

The cougar primarily feeds upon mammals: deer being the staple diet 77%, porcupine 9%, domestic animals 4%, beaver 4%, horses 2%, with miscellaneous mammals (sheep, goats, elk, moose, lynx and mice, etc.) and grasses rounding out its meals. Kills are often covered with leaves and provide several meals. Cougars hunt during daylight but become most active at dawn and dusk.

Habitat:

This wide ranging animal can effectively live from sea level to the alpine zone and from thick forests to open grassland. However, it now largely resides in the wild mountainous terrain of the Rockies westward.

The cougar, puma or mountain lion once occupying the entire continent is now primarily restricted in range to the wild rugged wilderness areas of the Rocky Mountains and western ranges. While still common in a few areas it is often persecuted as a cattle killer. Its hairy coat enables it to winter in the coldest countries.

Cougars are extremely shy, and fortunate is the person seeing the graceful king of the mountains move across a ridge or stalk a deer or rabbit. Prey is either stalked by scent and sight and pursued by a short fast run in which the cat is either quickly successful or he gives up; or the unsuspecting prey is pounced upon as it passes a silently waiting cat.

While deer are the main prey species, the cougar hunt rabbits, coyotes, beaver, sheep, goats and other creatures.

Cougars have very keen sense of smell—here cat is checking photographer's tracks

Juvenile cougars are taught to hunt from five months of age. They are abandoned at 12-18 months when about three-quarters grown to find their own territory. During this learning phase and while searching for an unoccupied territory young males most often get into difficulty with farmers and ranchers.

A stretch

LYNX
Lynx lynx

Vital Statistics:

Weight (pounds):
At birth	½
Adult male	24 (15 - 35)
Adult female	20 (12 - 26)

Total length:
Adult male	35 in. (30 - 42)
Adult female	33 in. (30 - 38)

Reproduction:

Lynx populations fluctuate greatly around the 10 year varying hare cycle. The peak and crash of the lynx population follows about one year behind that of its main food source, the hare. The one to six (average two to three) young are born in May to June, become independent by six to eight months, and mature at one year of age.

Food:

The lynx is a nocturnal hunter, preying primarily upon varying hares, grouse, mice and carrion. In the "crash" years of the hares, lynx often disperse southward from their northern boreal forest wilderness and in a desperate search for food frequently get into trouble with chicken farmers.

Habitat:

The lynx is primarily a forest dweller.

Lynx kitten

Lynx eating
from road kill

On the lookout!

The lynx is a solitary hunter of the night. The long soft gray coat unfortunately is in great demand for trimming fur parkas and in recent years there has been an upsurge in interest in trapping because of the higher fur prices. However, the wilderness home of the boreal forest still affords protection to a large number of lynx.

Lynx bedded down in snow
between feeds at nearby kill

WOLF
Canis lupus

Vital Statistics:

Weight (pounds):
At birth	1½ - 2
Adult male	100 (80 - 175)
Adult female	85 (65 - 130)

Total length:
Adult male	65 - 73 in.
Adult female	58 - 65 in.

Shoulder height:
Adult male	30 - 38 in.
Adult female	26 - 34 in.

Food:

The wolf is primarily a hunter of big game: deer, elk, moose, sheep and caribou being the staple species where abundant. Smaller mammals and birds are also important. Quantitative studies have shown the wolves primarily prey upon the young, aged or sick animals.

Habitat:

Wolves inhabit every niche from open plains to deep forest.

Reproduction:

Wolves presumably mate for life. Peak mating occurs during the two weeks around the beginning of March, with pupping peaking 60 to 63 days later. More than a dozen pups in a litter have been recorded, but seven is average. Pups start to join in on hunting expeditions by September. Females are mature at two while males mature at three years of age.

The howl

The wolf is a tireless runner, capable of sustained chase over several miles. Cooperative pack action assists in bringing down prey or subduing larger animals like moose and elk. Strong, vigorous, healthy prey can usually ward off attacking wolves or outrun them.

The wild snowblown wilderness—the wolf's domain

Three-month-old wolf pup

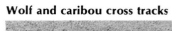

Wolf and caribou cross tracks

Young moose held at bay by two wolves

Deep snow or weakness through starvation handicaps the prey and enables the predator to fulfill his roll of selector of the weak and controller of prey in overabundance.

The enormously strong jaws enable the wolf to quickly dispatch its prey or break the long bones for the nutritive marrow.

Contrary to popular belief there is not a single authenticated record of wolves ever killing a man. On the contrary to his maligned personality, the wolves have strong family ties and sense enough to avoid man whenever possible.

Wolves finishing off a moose carcass

... and elk

COYOTE
Canis latrans

Vital Statistics:

Weight (pounds):
At birth	½
Adult male	35
Adult female	23

Total length:
Adult male	45 - 73 in.
Adult female	42 - 47 in.

Food:

About one-third of the diet is made up of hares and cottontail rabbits and another one-third of carrion. The balance is a wide variety of small mammals, birds, insects, etc., with mice being dominant, though poultry plays an important role with some individuals.

Habitat:

The versatile coyote prefers open forests and grasslands and can be found from valley bottoms to alpine tundra.

Reproduction:

The coyote is only sexually active from late January to late March and after a gestation of 60 to 63 days gives birth to three to ten young (average six). The young become self-sufficient at six to nine months but don't become sexually mature until one and one-half to two years.

The coyote's evening and early morning howls are familiar to all living in coyote country. Its scientific name 'Canis latrans' means 'barking dog'. In recent years the coyote has learned to live off and around man's abode. They have become beggars throughout many of the National Parks and have learned to scavenge garbage right within many city limits.

The coyote is omnivorous, either catching prey (73%), scrounging carrion (25%) or seeking out vegetation (2%). Cottontails, snowshoe hares and small rodents constitute most of this prey though through pack cooperation they can occasionally kill deer, antelope or sheep. While they will chase foxes and the bobcats they must avoid becoming meals for wolves, cougars, bears and even golden eagles. There are several accounts of single coyotes chasing deer and sheep only to have the would-be prey turn around and run the coyote out of the country

Alert to sights and sounds

Coyotes squabble over winter kill while ravens have feast

Poison victims

Roadside scrounger

On the hunt

Thick and heavy winter coat insulates coyote from cold

This coyote had just crossed stream on its hunt for beaver kits and mice

Four-month-old coyote pups

Coyotes have been known to have up to 19 young in a litter but 5 to 7 pups are most common. Both parents feed and care for the pups who are born from late April to early May. They are not sexually mature until just prior to reaching two years of age

Snow on nose is from routing under snow for mice and voles

RED FOX
Vulpes vulpes

Vital Statistics:

Weight (pounds):

At birth	¼
Adult male	10 (9 - 15)
Adult female	8 (7 - 10)

Total length:

Adult male	40 - 46 in.
Adult female	36 - 42 in.

Food:

The red fox is omnivorous with a strong preference for meats. These are primarily small mammals: mice, ground squirrels, moles, muskrats, cottontails and hares. An assortment of birds, insects and a very wide variety of vegetation, including berries, corn, grasses, apples, etc., make up its fare.

Habitat:

Red foxes prefer the forest openings and edges and along lakeshores or streambeds.

Reproduction:

The three to ten young are born from March to May after a 49 to 53 day gestation period. The pups appear above ground at one month, become independent at 15 weeks and become sexually mature at one year.

Red foxes are omnivorous, selecting much vegetation or invertebrates during the summer and mainly meat in winter. Birds and invertebrates each make up about 25 percent of the diet with small mammals—mice, moles, ground squirrels, cottontails and varying hares, etc., making up the other half. Foxes in turn are preyed upon by golden eagles, coyotes and lynx.

The pelage comes in three color phases—the basic red fox, the cross fox, which is browner with darker hairs across shoulder forming a cross, and the rare silver fox which has black fur with silver tips on its guard hairs

Red fox closes on varying hare

Red Fox

Fox pups less than two weeks of age

Fox pups at den

Large pups play stalking games

The young pups are weaned at one month and start to play around the den entrance. Home life is short and by four months of age they abandon the family unit to fend for themselves. The young, born from March to May, are sexually mature at 10 months. They breed from January to March in time to have their first litter on their first birthday. Since the average litter size is 5 young, they can quickly build up their numbers.

Three-month-old pups are nearing independence

Fox pups at den entrance

LONG-TAILED WEASEL
Mustela frenata

Vital Statistics:

Weight:
Females	3 - 4 oz.
Males	6 - 9 oz.

Length:
Females	16 in.
Males	18 in.

Reproduction:

Breeding season	July - August
Birth season	March to May
Gestation period	220 - 337 days
Litter size	6 (3 - 9)

Food:

This little weasel primarily feeds upon meadow voles, deer mice, chipmunks, pocket gophers, ground squirrels and prairie dogs though any small vertebrate or invertebrate will be taken. Little vegetation is consumed.

Habitat:

The long-tailed weasel frequents waterways in open grassland, parklands and the open alpine meadows.

MARTEN
Martes americana

Vital Statistics:

Weight:	
Females	1½ lb.
Males	2½ lb.
Length:	
Females	22 in.
Males	24 in.

Reproduction:

Breeding season	July - August
Birth season	March - April
Gestation period	8½ - 9 months
Litter size	3 (2 - 6)

Food:

Mice (65%) and squirrels (10%) are the staple food though any small animal is potential food. Considerable berries are eaten during the summer.

Habitat:

This specialist is restricted to the climax (mature and long standing) coniferous forest.

Martens argue over possession of freshly caught squirrel

Marten eating mouse

Marten

Marten chasing squirrel

FISHER

Martes pennanti

Vital Statistics:

Weight:
Female	5 - 6 lb.
Male	8 - 10 lb.

Length:
Female	35 in.
Male	41 in.

Reproduction:

Breeding season	March - April
Birth season	March
Gestation period	340 - 360 days
Litter size	2.5 (1-5)

Food:

Eighty percent of the fisher's diet is meat with squirrels, voles, varying hares, mice and porcupine being the dominant species. The fisher has learned how to make an attack on the unprotected belly of the porcupine. Some carrion, birds and an assortment of vegetation is also consumed.

Habitat:

The fisher lives in the coniferous and deciduous forest usually around waterways.

Fisher

Young fisher

WOLVERINE
Gulo gulo

Vital Statistics:

Weight:
Females	22 lb.
Males	32 lb.

Length:
Females	35 in.
Males	40 in.

Reproduction:

Breeding season	May - June
Birth season	February - April
Gestation period	7 - 8 months
Litter size	2.5 (1.5)

Food:

The wolverine is primarily a scavenger living on winter kills and prey caught by wolves, lynx or bears. They also capture deer—it is believed by dropping onto them from trees. A wide range of vegetation is also consumed along with a variety of smaller mammals (beaver, mice, porcupine, etc.), birds and even fish.

Habitat:

The wolverine is a mammal of the boreal forest and subalpine to alpine zones but also follows herds of caribou out onto the tundra.

Wolverine, while largely ground-dwellers, are agile climbers

RIVER OTTER
Lontra canadensis

Vital Statistics:

Weight:
Female	16 lb.
Male	18 lb.

Length:
Female	44 in.
Male	46 in.

Reproduction:

Breeding season	February - March
Birth season	March - April
Gestation period	9½ - 12½ months
Litter size	3 (1 - 5)

Food:

The river or land otter specializes in catching its food underwater. Inland over 90% of this is fish: minnows, sunfish, catfish, sculpins, perch and trout. Invertebrates, amphibians and even muskrats or birds will be taken. On the seacoast many additional marine invertebrates are consumed.

Habitat:

Riparian to the extreme, the otter is seldom found away from a waterway whether at sea level or in an alpine glacial pool.

River or land otter

MINK
Mustela vison

Vital Statistics:

Weight:
Females	1 1/3 lb.
Males	2½ lb.

Length:
Females	19 in.
Males	23 in.

Reproduction:

Breeding season	February - March
Birth season	April - May
Gestation period	50 (40 - 75) days
Litter size	5 (3 - 10)

Food:

Small mammals and fish make up about one-third of the mink's diet with amphibians, reptiles, birds, insects and worms filling out this active predator's prey. In some areas the muskrats form the major item, in others it might be voles. Minnows, dace and shiners are the favored fish species.

Habitat:

Mink are riparian, frequenting the forest edges of streams, rivers, ponds, lakes and seashore.

Mink are excellent swimmers but hunt small mammals, birds and invertebrates around shoreline

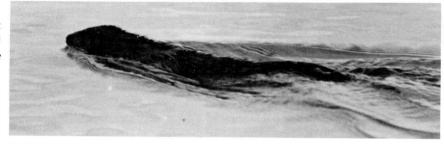

BADGER

Taxidea taxus

Vital Statistics:

Weight:
Females	14 lb.
Males	25 lb.

Length:
Females	24 in.
Males	32 in.

Reproduction:

Breeding season	August - September
Birth season	May - June
Gestation period	7 - 9 months
Litter size	3 (2 - 5)

Food:

The badger is largely a specialized feeder—its large claws being adapted for digging small mammals out of their burrows. Ground squirrels, pocket gophers, prairie dogs and other small rodents are the prime prey though ground nesting birds, eggs, and many insects and reptiles are eaten as well.

Habitat:

Badgers live in open country or in clearings in dryer areas.

Badger

...the end of a snake

The fossorial badger lives in holes he adeptly digs with his powerful clawed paws

Strong, powerful jaws can quickly dispatch ground squirrels

STRIPED SKUNK
Mephitis mephitis

Vital Statistics:

Weight:
Female	3 lb.
Male	4 lb.

Length:
Female	22 in.
Male	23 in.

Reproduction:

Breeding season	February - March
Birth season	May
Gestation period	63 days
Litter size	5 (2 - 10)

Food:

The skunk is a true omnivore, opportunistically feeding upon whatever is available, whether it be carrion, birds' eggs, insects, small mammals, grasses or succulent berries or frogs and fish.

Habitat:

The striped skunk prefers well hedged agricultural land or open forests and river bottoms.

Mother and baby **Striped skunk spraying**

SPOTTED SKUNK
Spilogale garcilis

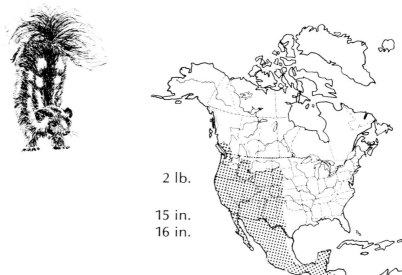

Vital Statistics:

Weight	2 lb.
Length:	
Female	15 in.
Male	16 in.

Reproduction:

Breeding season	November - December
Birth season	March - April
Gestation period	121 days
Litter size	4 (2 - 8)

Food:

The spotted skunk is primarily carnivorous though relishes berries, grapes and corn, etc., in season. The bulk of the winter and spring diet consists of cottontails, voles, rats, mice, reptiles, amphibians, insects, eggs and even carrion.

Habitat:

This is the common skunk of farmlands and dryer scrublands. It avoids thick forests and wet areas. Skunks are not true hibernators but several may den up together in cold weather.

The spotted skunk can spew its pungent musk 6-12 feet. When threatened it first raises its tail then does a handstand, often approaching adversary and if still intimidated it will then spray

PIKA
Ochotona princeps

Vital Statistics:

Average weight (adult)	5 - 9 oz.
Average length (adult)	7 - 8 in.
Winter color	gray - brown

Reproduction:

Breeding age of females	1 year
Litters per year	2
Litter size	3 (1 - 6)
Gestation period (days)	30
Breeding season	April - July

Food:

In the restricted alpine environment almost every plant is eaten, with grasses, sedges, lupines, paintbrush and willows being but a few. These grasses are sun dried to cure them and then stored underground in chambers, sometimes surrounded by ice, to be eaten throughout winter as the pika does not hibernate.

Habitat:

Pikas live in talus slopes and in rock piles usually above timberline in the alpine zone but occasionally into the forested areas if there is sufficient rocky habitat. In winter they are active below the snow cover in the rock piles.

Pika in his rocky mountain domain

The alarm call

Busy pika gathers and stores flowers and
grasses for his winter food supply

MOUNTAIN COTTONTAIL

Sylviagus nuttalli

Vital Statistics:

Average weight (adult)	2.0 - 3.3 lb.
Average length (adult)	14 - 16 in.
Winter color	gray - brown

Reproduction:

Breeding age of females	8 - 10 mo.
Litters per year	3 - 5
Litter size	4.3 (1 - 6)
Gestation period (days)	28 - 30
Breeding season	March - July

Food:

Cottontails are largely crepuscular, feeding mainly at dusk and dawn. The spring and summer food is a very wide variety of herbs and grasses while the winter fare consists of buds of shrubs, twigs and young trees. The nutritive cambium layer provides much nourishment in winter.

Habitat:

The cottontail prefers dry open areas with an abundance of scattered cover. Ground squirrel and badger holes are often used for shelter.

Cottontail nest

Like the rest of the rabbit family the cotton-tails are active all winter but do not turn white like most of the varying hares or some of the jack rabbits 97

SNOWSHOE HARE

Lepus americanus

Vital Statistics:

Average weight (adult)	2.5 - 4.0 lb.
Average length (adult)	17 - 19 in.
Winter color	white

Reproduction:

Breeding age of females	1 yr.
Litters per year	3 - 4
Litter size	3.5 (2-7)
Gestation period (days)	36 - 37
Breeding season	March - August

Food:

In summer succulent grasses and many herbs are eaten along with leaves of trembling aspen, birch and willow. In winter their fare is the buds, twigs and branches of many shrubs and trees. As the snow deepens they can reach higher and higher by standing on the frozen crust.

Habitat:

This hare prefers the thickets and heavy coniferous and deciduous forests from which it works outward for feeding in the more open areas.

Young varying hare

98

Snowshoe or varying hare varies its coat between brown in summer and white in winter

The large feet of snowshoe hare enable it to more easily walk on snow

By standing on long legs they can reach high up for nutritious shoots or leaves

WHITE-TAILED JACK RABBIT

Lepus townsendii

Vital Statistics:

Average weight (adult)	6.5 - 12 lb.
Average length (adult)	20 - 26 in.
Winter color	white

Reproduction:

Breeding age of females	1 yr.
Litters per year	3 - 4
Litter size	5 (1 - 9)
Gestation period (days)	28 - 30
Breeding season	March - July

Food:

Grasses and clover are favored summer fare with buds and the bark of trees and shrubs forming most of the winter food.

Habitat:

White-tailed jack rabbits favor the open sagebrush plains and pasture land and only seek shelter during blizzars in forest cover. In the mountainous areas they will penetrate the open pine-juniper forests.

White-tail jack rabbit in winter pelage

Jack rabbit in sage brush

Jack rabbit partially in white winter pelage

Jack rabbit

HOARY MARMOT
Marmota caligata

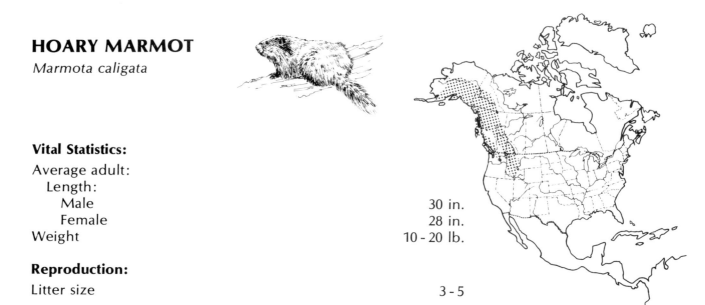

Vital Statistics:

Average adult:	
Length:	
Male	30 in.
Female	28 in.
Weight	10 - 20 lb.

Reproduction:

Litter size	3 - 5

Habitat:

Boulder strewn alpine slopes and rocky openings in subalpine forest

Hoary marmot

YELLOW-BELLIED MARMOT
Marmota flaviventris

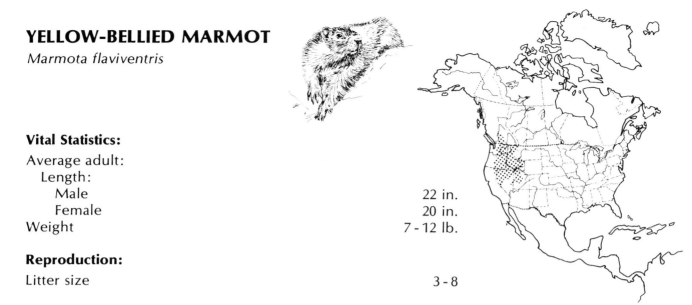

Vital Statistics:

Average adult:
  Length:
    Male   22 in.
    Female   20 in.
Weight   7 - 12 lb.

Reproduction:

Litter size   3 - 8

Habitat:

Dry, rocky valleys and slopes in the north, but extends into alpine zone from Wyoming southward.

Yellow-bellied marmot

WOODCHUCK
Marmota monax

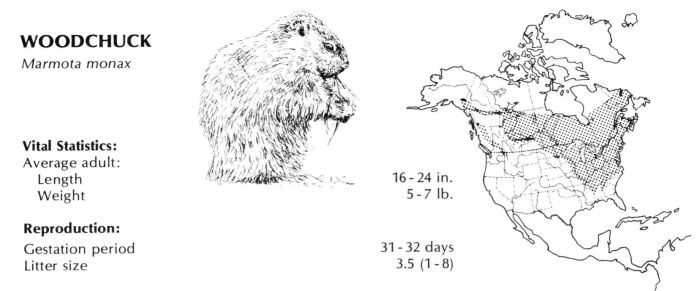

Vital Statistics:
Average adult:
  Length   16 - 24 in.
  Weight   5 - 7 lb.

Reproduction:

Gestation period   31 - 32 days
Litter size   3.5 (1 - 8)

Habitat:
Open woodlots, pastures and fence rows, particularly where buildings and stumps occur. This animal has greatly benefitted from agricultural practices which have opened up the land.

Woodchuck

RICHARDSON'S GROUND SQUIRREL

Spermophilus richardsonii

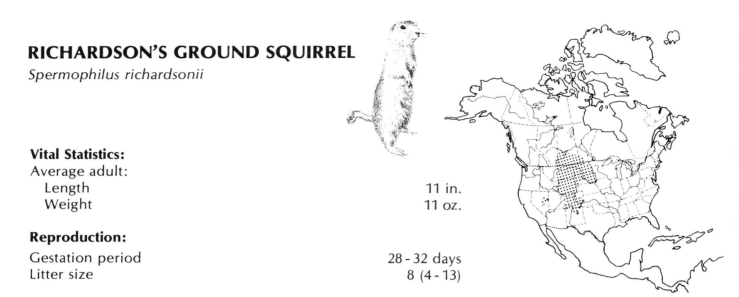

Vital Statistics:

Average adult:
  Length   11 in.
  Weight   11 oz.

Reproduction:

Gestation period   28 - 32 days
Litter size   8 (4 - 13)

Habitat:

Sage plains and grasslands from 5,000 ft. to above timberline. Also openings in montane forest in Wyoming and Colorado.

Female and young at burrow entrance—ready to disappear at first sign of danger

Richardson's ground squirrel

The Richardson's ground squirrel largely inhabits the open prairies or high rolling hills where it lives in loose colonies. Its habit of standing erect when disturbed earned it the name 'picket pin'

Richardson's ground squirrel eats from carcass of road-killed neighbor

107

COLUMBIAN GROUND SQUIRREL
Spermophilus columbianus

Vital Statistics:

Average adult:

Length	14 in.
Weight	17 oz.

Reproduction:

Gestation period	24 days
Litter size	3.5 (2 - 7)

Habitat:

Meadows, forest openings and alpine parks. Usually colonial.

Young Columbian ground squirrel eats a wild rose

The Columbian ground squirrel is one of the largest and most beautiful of the ground squirrels and often chooses equally beautiful surroundings in which to live

BLACK-TAILED PRAIRIE DOG
Cynomys ludovicianus

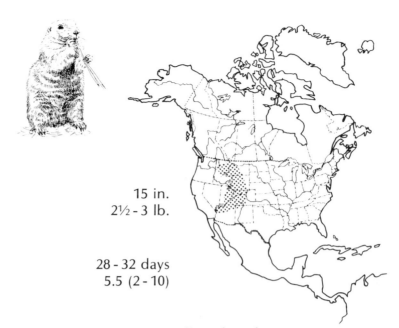

Vital Statistics:

Average adult:
Length   15 in.
Weight   2½ - 3 lb.

Reproduction:

Geatation period   28 - 32 days
Litter size   5.5 (2 - 10)

Habitat:

Grassy mountain "parks" from 6,000 to 12,000 foot elevation. Usually colonial.

Prairie dogs are distinguished from the closely related ground squirrels by being larger in size, stouter bodied, shorter tailed and with very short ears, often hidden in the fur

110

THIRTEEN LINED GROUND SQUIRREL

Spermophilus tridecemlineatus

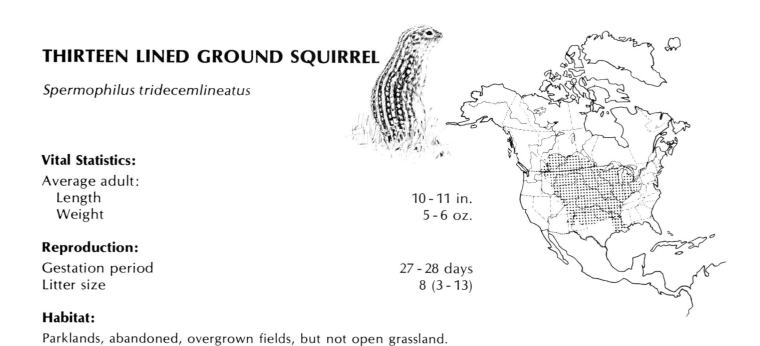

Vital Statistics:

Average adult:
Length 10 - 11 in.
Weight 5 - 6 oz.

Reproduction:

Gestation period 27 - 28 days
Litter size 8 (3 - 13)

Habitat:

Parklands, abandoned, overgrown fields, but not open grassland.

Thirteen-lined ground squirrel

GOLDEN-MANTLED GROUND SQUIRREL
Spermophilus lateralis

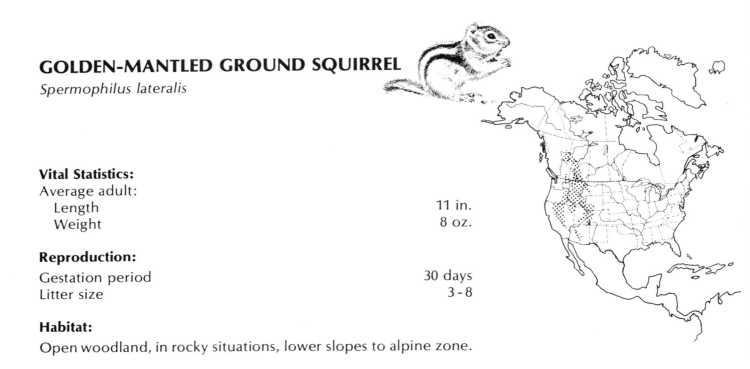

Vital Statistics:

Average adult:

Length	11 in.
Weight	8 oz.

Reproduction:

Gestation period	30 days
Litter size	3 - 8

Habitat:

Open woodland, in rocky situations, lower slopes to alpine zone.

Golden-mantled ground squirrel emerges from burrow in the alpine zone

The golden-mantled ground squirrel is one of the best known and most beautifully marked ground squirrels. It frequents many campsites throughout the Rockies, commonly begs for handouts

YELLOW PINE CHIPMUNK
Eutamias amoenus

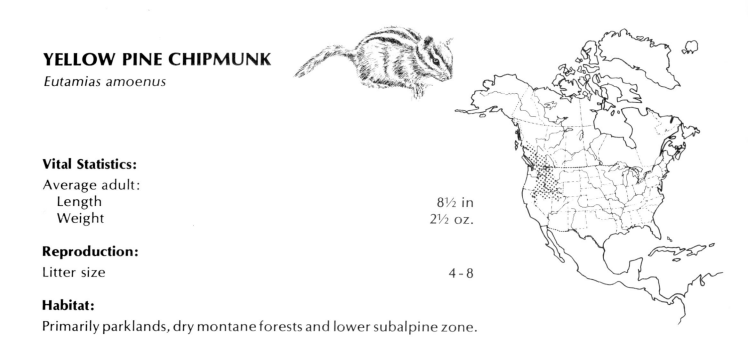

Vital Statistics:

Average adult:
Length	8½ in
Weight	2½ oz.

Reproduction:

Litter size	4 - 8

Habitat:

Primarily parklands, dry montane forests and lower subalpine zone.

Yellow pine or northwestern chipmunk

Mother chipmunk attends 10 day old young

The chipmunk is usually the first animal to make its presence known around a new campsite, as it darts back and forth along logs or climbs the lower branches of nearby trees, often carrying its tail vertically. The nest is underground, where the animal will undergo a light hibernation during the coldest months

FLYING SQUIRREL

Glaucomys sabrinus

Vital Statistics:

Average adult:

Length	12½ in.
Weight	5 - 6 oz.

Reproduction:

Gestation period	37-40 days
Litter size	3 - 6

Habitat:

Well forested mountain slopes with fairly mature tree growth.

The northern flying squirrel

116

The most outstanding feature of the flying squirrel is the loosely fitting skin, that is extended in a broad fold from each side between the foreleg and the hind leg. By extending the legs a planing surface is formed on which the squirrel may glide or parachute from higher to lower places. This is not truely flight, as with the bats. The flying squirrel is strictly nocturnal, although it might be seen in daylight, when disturbed from the nest

RED (SPRUCE) SQUIRREL
Tamiasciurus hudsonicus

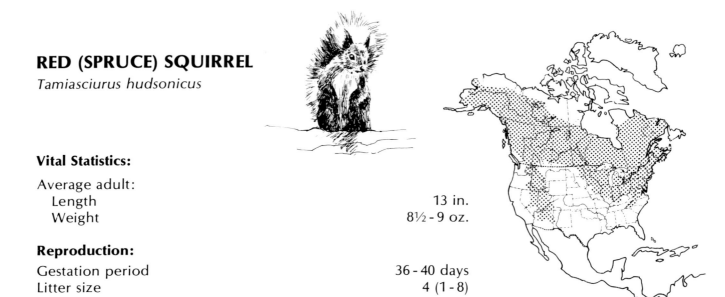

Vital Statistics:

Average adult:
Length	13 in.
Weight	8½ - 9 oz.

Reproduction:
Gestation period	36 - 40 days
Litter size	4 (1 - 8)

Habitat:

Fairly dense coniferous forests of the montane and subalpine zones.

Often heard giving its scolding warning calls before it is seen, this highly arboreal squirrel is active all winter long making short forays from its bulky stick nest to food caches

BEAVER

Castor canadensis

Vital Statistics:

Weight:
Adult male	25 - 55 lb.
Adult female	25 - 55 lb.

Total length:
Adult male	38 (36 - 43) in.
Adult female	36 (34 - 40) in.

Reproduction:

Mating season	winter
Gestation period	90 - 110 days
Litter size	3 (1 - 7)
Age at first reproduction	2 yrs.
Litter per year	1

Food:

In summer, pond succulents such as water-lillies, cattails, and duckweed, are the main fare supplemented with leaves, buds and some bark of trees. In winter the highly nutritious cambium layer become the staple food. Trembling aspen is favored but a variety of trees are consumed. These include willows, birch, cottonwood, poplar, and occasionally pine and spruce. It is estimated that one acre of aspen will keep one beaver one year. Food is eaten underwater or in the hut.

Habitat:

Beavers inhabit lakes, ponds and slow moving streams that are surrounded by trees.

119

Beaver cuttings

Beaver community

The beaver, exploited for its valuable fur, played an important role in the exploitation and settlement of northern North America, and earned itself the distinction of being Canada's national emblem. Beaver country is readily identified by the beaver's dams, lodges and tree cuttings. The dams must impound water sufficiently deep that it doesn't freeze through so the beavers can swim underwater in winter to collect food from their storage areas.

Beaver swimming with cutting

Beaver cutting a tree

Beaver dam in Waterton National Park

Young beaver on top of lodge

Beaver chewing bark

MUSKRAT

Ondatra zibethicus

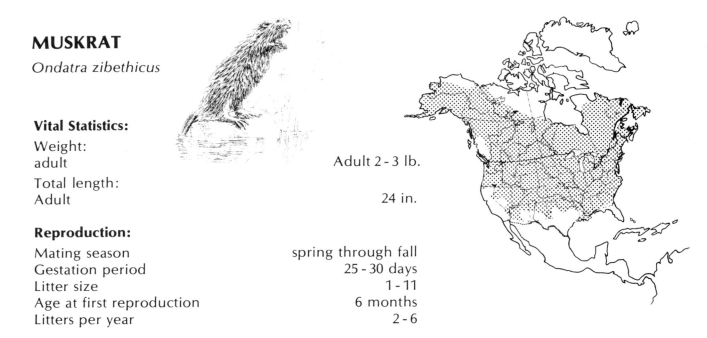

Vital Statistics:

Weight:
adult   Adult 2 - 3 lb.

Total length:
Adult   24 in.

Reproduction:

Mating season	spring through fall
Gestation period	25 - 30 days
Litter size	1 - 11
Age at first reproduction	6 months
Litters per year	2 - 6

Food:

Summer food is mainly emergent vegetation such as bulrushes, cattails, sedge and water lilies, while winter food is mainly submerged vegetation (so it isn't frozen) such as water lily tubers, bladderwort, etc. Fresh-water mussels, frogs, salamanders and even catfish are consumed.

Habitat:

Muskrats live in slow moving water that does not freeze over in winter.

Muskrat feeding on pond weeds

Muskrat house built with succulent vegetation

Muskrat habitat

PORCUPINE

Erethizon dorsatum

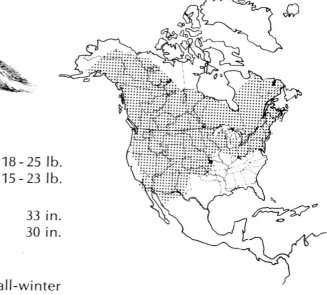

Vital Statistics:

Weight:
Adult male	18 - 25 lb.
Adult female	15 - 23 lb.

Total length:
Adult male	33 in.
Adult female	30 in.

Reproduction:

Mating season	late fall-winter
Gestation period	110 - 120 days
Litter size	1 - 2
Litters per year	1

Food:

The porcupine is a vegetarian, primarily living during summer on the leaves of many shrubs and trees or on grasses, pond lily or even corn. In winter it feeds upon the highly nutritive cambium layer of a variety of coniferous and deciduous trees. Antlers, road signs and human implements are chewed for their mineral and salt content.

Habitat:

The porcupine primarily inhabits the forest, either coniferous or deciduous, but will venture out into open grassland during summer.

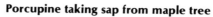

Yellow-haired porcupine in tree   **Porcupine taking sap from maple tree**

Also in a treeless country one might encounter a porky

Contrary to popular belief porcupines cannot throw their quills but rather they easily detach upon contact, leaving a pained tormentor.

Young porcupines are born well advanced with eyes open and the ability to run and follow mother immediately but they don't become sexually mature until two and a half years later.

125

DEER MOUSE
Peromyscus maniculatus

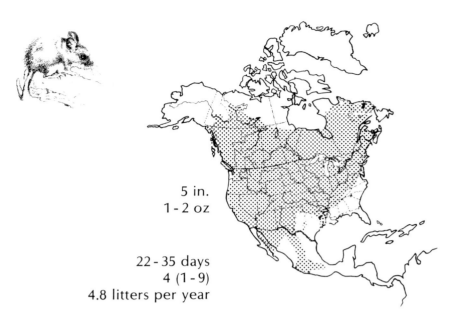

Vital Statistics:

Adverage adult:
    Length   5 in.
    Weight   1 - 2 oz

Reproduction:

Getation period   22 - 35 days
Litter size   4 (1 - 9)
                       4.8 litters per year

Habitat:

Tolerates extremely wide range of habitat from grassland to dark coniferous forests.

MISCELLANEOUS SMALL MAMMALS

Species	Distribution in Rockies	Usual Habitats
Masked shrew	South to northern New Mexico. Common.	Moist habitats in forested and alpine zones. Usually wet meadows and willow thickets.
Wandering shrew	South to Mexico. Common.	Moist situation in forested zones. 5,300 to 11,400 feet in Colorado.
Water shrew	South to northern New Mexico. Rare.	Most commonly along streams or ponds in dense spruce-fir forest.
Pygmy shrew	South to north-central Colorado. Rare.	Moist meadows, forest-meadow transition, and conifer forest.
Northern pocket gopher	Southeast B.C. amd southwest Alta. to northern New Mexico.	Open areas, usually sand soils, valley floor upward. Reaches Alpine zone in Colorado.
Bushy-tailed wood rat	South to northern New Mexico. Common.	Lower canyons to Alpine zone. Prefer dry, rocky forest land. Often use cabins, caves and mineshafts.
Northern bog lemming	Boreal. South to Glacier Park, Montana. Rare.	Black spruce and sphagnum bogs and soggy lake edges in coniferous forests to timberline and above.
Heather vole	South to extreme northern New Mexico. Scarce.	Wet sites in forest, particularly streamsides. Also common under lodgepole pine forest.
Red-backed vole	South to central New Mexico. Locally common.	Coniferous forests. Most abundant under lodgepole pine or aspen. 8,000 to 11,000 feet in Colorado.
Meadow vole	South to northern New Mexico. Periodically abundant.	Boggy places edges of springs. Wet meadows near permanent water. Wide elevational range.
Water vole	South to northeast Utah and southwest Wyoming. Rare.	High elevations. Banks of cold mountain streams and ponds above and below timberline.
Mountain vole	From west central Montana and northern Idaho, south to northwest Mexico.	Moist meadows and dry grassy areas, often under aspen. 6,000 feet in Colorado.
Long-tailed vole	South to southern New Mexico. Fairly common.	Streamside meadows and open forest. 5,000 feet to well above timberline in Colorado.
Western jumping mouse	South to central New Mexico. Fairly rare.	Moist areas, particularly streamside willows and lush growth under aspens.

PHOTO CREDITS

PART I

P2:DSH; P8: TWH; P10: NP, Np; P11: Np; P12: NP, Np; P13: NP; P14: NP, NP, NP, DD, DSH, NP; P15: NP, DD, DD, TW, DD; P16: NP; P17: TWH; P18: NP, TWH, TWH, TWH; P19: NP, NP, TW; P20; TWH, ONR, NP, TWH; P21: DB; P22:TI,TWH;P23:EK TWH, TWH, TWH; P24: DD; P25: TI, TI, TWH, NP; P26: NP, TI; P27: EK, TWH, EK, TWH; P28: DSH, TWH, TWH, TWH, TWH, TWH, TWH; P29: TWH, TWH, TWH, TWH, TI, TI, NP ; P30: ONR, TWH, ONR; P31: DSH; P32: DSH, P34: DSH, NP, TWH; P35: NP, NP; P36: TWH, TWH, TWH; P37: TWH, TWH, TWH, TWH, TWH; P38: TWH, TWH, TWH; P39: TWH, TWH, TWH, TWH, TWH; P40: TWH, EK TWH,TWH,TWH,TWH;P41:TWH; P42: DSH, TWH, NP, TWH; P43: TWH; P44: TWH, TWH, TWH; P45: DSH, TWH; P46: TWH, TWH, TWH; P47: TWH, TWH, TWH; P48: TWH, TWH, TWH, TWH; P49: TWH, TWH; P50: TWH, TWH, TWH, TWH; P51: TWH, TWH, TWH; P52: TWH, TWH, TWH, TWH, TWH, TWH; P53: TWH, TWH, TWH, TWH; P54: TWH, TWH; P55: TWH, TWH; P56: TWH; P57: TWH, TWH, TWH, DSH, TWH, TWH; P58: DSH, JB, TWH, TWH; P59: TWH, TWH, TWH, TWH, TWH, TWH; P60: TWH, TWH, TWH; P61: TWH, TWH, TWH, TWH, TWH, TWH; P62: DSH, TWH, TWH; P63: TWH, TWH, TWH, DSH, TWH; P64: TWH, TWH, TWH; P65: TWH; P66: TWH, TWH, TWH, TWH; P67: TWH, TWH; P68: TWH, TWH, TWH, TWH; P69: ONR, DB, LRH, TWH, EK; P70: LRH, TWH, LRH, TWH, TWH, EK; P71: TWH, TWH, TWH, TWH; P72: TWH, TWH, TWH, TWH; P73: TWH, TI, TWH, EK, EK; P74: TWH, TWH, EK, TWH; P75: LRH, EK; P76: TWH, TWH; P77: TWH, TWH, TWH, AG, TWH; P78: EK; P80: TWH, TWH, TWH; P81: NP, AG; P82: TWH; P83: BH, DSH; P84: TI, TWH, TWH; P85: IF, DSH; P86: TWH, TWH, TWH; P87: TWH, TWH, ONR; P88: TWH, ONR, TWH, TWH; P89: TI, TWH, NP; P90: TWH, TWH, DSH; P91: TWH, TWH, TWH, TWH; P93: TWH, TWH, TWH; P94: NP, NP, TWH; P95: AG, ONR; P96: NP; P97: TWH, BP, NP; P98: TWH; P99: DD, DSH; P101: TW, TW; P102: NP, AG; P103: TWH;

P105: DSH, DSH; P106: TI; P107: TWH, DSH, TWH; P108: TWH, DSH, TWH; P109: TWH, TWH, TWH, TWH; P110: TWH; P111: DD, DSH; P112: JC; P113: TWH, AG; P114: KM; P115: TWH, TWH, AG; P116: TWH, TWH, TWH; P117: ONR, TWH, TWH; P119: TWH, DSH, TWH; P120: NP;P121:TWH;P123: SWK NP;P124: KM,TWH; P125: TWH, TWH, AG, NM; P126: KM, TW; P127: TWH; P128: NP; P131: TWH; P132: TWH, ONR; P133: TWH, TWH,KM; P134: TWH, TWH, TWH, TWH, TWH; P135: TWH, ONR, TI; P136: DD, NP; P137: DSH; P138: TWH, TWH, TWH, TWH, TWH; P139: DSH, DSH, TWH, TWH, TWH, TWH, TWH; P140: TWH, TWH, TWH; P141: TWH, TWH; P143: PP; P144: ONR; P145: KM; P146: WT, TWH, TWH, KM; P147: CR, TWH, DSH, TI, NM; P148: EJ, TWH, AG; P149: EH, KM; P150: DSH, ONR, DSH, DSH, DSH; P151: TWH, DSH, KM; P152: TWH, TWH, GJ; P153: VC, TWH; P156: PP; P157: TWH, TWH, VC; P158: TWH, TWH, TWH; P159: TWH, TWH; P160: TWH, TWH, TWH, TWH; P161: TWH, TWH, TWH, TWH; P162: TWH, DSH, DSH, TWH, TWH, BP; P164: ONR, TWH, VC, TWH; P165: VC, TWH, TWH; P166: TWH, TWH, TWH; P167: KM.

PART II

P4: NP; P5: TWH, TWH; P6: TWH, TWH, TWH; P7: TWH; P8: TWH, DSH; P9: TWH; P10: TWH; P11: TW, TWH; P12: TWH, TWH, TWH, TWH, TWH, TWH; P13: DSH; P14: TWH; P15: AG; P16: TWH, NP; P17: TWH; P18: TWH; P19: TWH; P20: TWH, DSH, TWH; P21: DSH, TWH, TWH; P22: TWH; P23: TWH, TWH, DSH; P24: TWH, NP, TWH, NP, ONR; P25: TWH, TWH, TWH, TWH, NP, NP; P26: TWH; P27: KM, TWH; P28: TWH, TWH, TWH, TWH; P29: TWH, TWH, TW, TWH; P30: TWH; P31: TWH, TWH, TWH; P32: TWH, ONR; P33: TWH, TWH, TWH; P34: TWH, ONR, ONR; P35: TWH, TWH, TWH; P36: TW; P37: TWH, TW, TWH, TWH, TW, TWH; P38: TWH; P39: TWH, ONR, TWH, TWH, TWH, TI, TWH; P40: DSH, TWH, TI, DSH; P41: DSH, DSH, DSH; P42: TWH, TWH, TWH, TWH, TWH; P43: TWH; P44: EK, TWH, TWH; P45: BP, TWH, EK; P46: LRH, LRH, TWH; P47: LRH, LRH, LRH, TWH; P48: TWH; P49: TWH, TWH; P50: TWH, TWH, TWH; P50: TWH, TWH, TWH; P51: TWH, TWH; P52: TWH, TWH, TWH; P53: TWH, TWH; P54: DSH, DSH, DSH; P55: DSH, DSH, DSH, TWH, DSH; P56: TWH, BP, NP; P57: JC; P58: TI; P59: TWH; P60: TWH, TWH, ONR, TWH, JC; P61: JC, JC; P62: TWH; P63: TWH; P64: TWH, JC; P65: ONR, TWH, TWH; P66: IF, ONR, DSH; P67: JC, TWH, TWH, TWH, NP, CZS; P68: DSH; P69: DSH; P70: TWH, TWH, TWH, TWH; P71: TWH, TWH; P72: TWH, TWH, TWH, TWH, TWH; P73: TWH, JC; P74: TWH, DSH, TWH, TWH, TWH; P75: TWH; P76: ONR; P77: TWH, TWH, TWH, IF; P78: TWH, TW; P79: TWH, ONR, TW, TW; P80: NM, TWH; P81: DD; P82: TWH; P83: IF; P84: TWH, IF, TI; P85: DSH, ONR, ONR; P86: IF; P87: TWH, P88: DSH, TWH, IF; P89: DSH; P90: TWH, DSH, DSH, TWH; P91: TW; P92: AG, IF; P93: TWH, BP; P94: TWH; P95: TWH, TWH; P96: SWK; P97: ONR, TW; P98: DSH, KM; P99: NP, ONR, ONR; P100: NP; P101: TWH, NP, DD; P102: TWH; P103: TW; P104: TWH, P105: BP; P106: TW; P107: AC, TW, TWH, KM, KM; P108: TWH, TWH, DSH; P109: DSH, KM, TWH; P110: TWH, DSH; P111: KM; P112: DSH; P113: TWH, TWH, TWH; P114: TWH; P114: TWH; P115: TWH, TWH, TWH; P116: TWH; P117: NM, NM, IF, NP, ONR; P118: TWH, TWH; P119: TWH; P120: NP, TI, IF, IF; P121: AG, ONR, IF; P122: TWH; P123: ONR, NP, DSH; P124: NM, ONR; P125: NM, TWH, IF, ONR, TWH; P126: TW.

INDEX